Joy
of
Cooking

Christmas
Cookies

by Irma S. Rombauer,
Marion Rombauer Becker and Ethan Becker

Color photographs by Maura McEvoy
Line drawings by Laura Hartman Maestro
Chapter-opening silhouette by Jacqueline Chwast

SCRIBNER

Scribner
1230 Avenue of the Americas
New York, NY 10020

SCRIBNER and design are trademarks of Simon & Schuster Inc.

Joy of Cooking is a trademark of The Joy of Cooking Trust

Designed by Margery Cantor
Set in Minion

Manufactured in the United States of America

1   3   5   7   9   10   8   6   4   2

Library of Congress Cataloging-in-Publication Data
Rombauer, Irma von Starkloff, date.
Joy of cooking Christmas cookies / by Irma S. Rombauer, Marion Rombauer Becker and Ethan Becker.
p.   cm.
Includes index.
1. Cookies. 2. Christmas cookery.   I. Becker, Marion Rombauer. II. Becker, Ethan. III. Title.
TX772.R65 1996
641.8'654—dc20   96-36388
CIP
ISBN 0-684-83357-3

CONTENTS

FOREWORD

I grew up in a house set on eight of the most beautiful acres that ever were, overlooking Clough Creek Valley in Newtown, just east of Cincinnati. Pop was an architect, and he designed the place, very much in the Bauhaus style. The folks called it Cockaigne, after the celebrated land of plenty in medieval myth—a land where, to quote one definition, "delicacies of food and drink were to be had for the taking." That certainly described our house, and never more so than at Christmastime.

For us, Christmas began with the purchase of the tree and the accompanying rituals. These started a week or so before Christmas at the Christmas tree lot at Forestvilie Fuel & Supply, where it seemed to take a cold, wet forever to select a tree and strap it to the top of our racy-looking 1953 Studebaker so we could get it home. Then, because Pop had an architect's eye for line and form, he would start reengineering the branches with wire and one thing or another to get absolute symmetry. And of course there always followed the traditional cursing of the Christmas tree stand.

Once the tree went up and stood there in its naked glory, the fun really started. Because my father was of the Bauhaus school, he was very much into the plain and straight and austere. But Christmas allowed him a certain delighted crazed indulgence, and he suddenly betrayed an Edwardian's appreciation for ornamentation and glitz. My brother and I were always full of childish wonder as all the familiar decorations got dragged out every year. We had everything from old home-baked salt-dough ornaments, some of which had been around for twenty or thirty years, to some beautiful delicate treasures that the folks had picked up in Mexico and some incredibly fine, almost gossamer-thin glass toadstools from Italy. When the tree was finally all dressed, it was a wonderful thing. And we always topped the evening off with cocoa and either a fudge feast or a praline bash. It was a night of wonderful excess.

Christmas Day at Cockaigne, like Christmas Days all over the country in those days, was devoted to the preparation and consumption of the Christmas feast. Most years at our house that feast was shared by a lot of people, because Mother tended to collect anybody who was stray and had no place else to eat on Christmas. Pop would always help cook the meal, in between stints fixing already mangled toys—and I recall his almost devilish delight in making the eggnog. This was his wintertime specialty, and it was an eggnog suitable for stunning oxen.

Our Christmas dinner table would be decorated with pine boughs cut from the trees that ringed our property, and there were always lots of candles. The centerpiece was the traditional turkey, perfectly roasted. The dressing tended to be mushroom. Twice-baked potatoes were a big thing some years; other years, the potatoes were mashed. Creamed spinach was usually present. Dessert was always a hazelnut or almond torte and plum pudding. Pop used to take all the leftover jams and preserves in the house and cook them up with cognac, then spoon this sort of syrup over the plum pudding, for which he had a great fondness.

The thing I remember about family dinners almost as much as I remember the great food is the great conversation. I come from a family that believed in ideas, big ideas, and our guests were also people of ideas. You might hear conversations about design and art, both ancient and modern, or about politics. The mention of philosophers and philosophy was not unheard of around our table.

After dinner came what Pop called the *Gescherung*, the sharing of gifts. The big family presents had been opened first thing in the morning, but there was always a little something for everybody who had shared dinner with us. It might be a book, or it might be a kitchen gadget. Mother had great enthusiasm for kitchen gadgets. When she found one she thought was really neat, she'd buy a case of them, and if you came to visit, you'd be hard pressed not to walk away with one.

Our Christmas dinner always ended with liqueurs and strong coffee for the grownups, and sometimes coffee for us kids, too, and then everybody would repair to the piano and Pop would pass out huge sheaves of sheet music on heavy paper, which he'd hand-copied and bound in ribbon over the years. He'd play and we'd all be happily forced to sing Christmas carols. Then we'd sit around the blazing fire and talk for a while longer before people went off into the night.

That was Christmas at Cockaigne. But from the time I was eight or nine, after Granny Rom had a stroke, we started spending our Christmases in St. Louis, where both my parents had come from originally. We had lots of relatives in St. Louis. There were always lots of other kids, and lots of Christmas trees, and there was a plethora of good food. It seemed as if almost everybody, on both sides of the family, was a good cook, and we were forever walking into this uncle's or that aunt's house to the smells of roasting hams and turkeys and baked goods of all kinds.

Strangely enough, when I think about my Christmases in St. Louis, one thing I have particularly strong memories of is cookies. The Rombauer side of the family is Hungarian, but the rest is solid German, and the cookies were always a combination of American and European styles. And there was never any shortage of them. One thing we *always* had were Christmas bars, made with chocolate, pecans, and molasses and various spices, both with lemon icing and without—because we all loved the lemon, but Mother was allergic to it. If I remember correctly, a couple of years she made some with orange juice and those were tasty as well. Some years there were Lebkuchen, some years there were Pfeffernüsse—and almost all years there were brownies wrapped with festive aluminum foil. On a few Christmases, I remember that Mom made anise-flavored, elaborately shaped Springerle. My brother Mark and I would be sent to mine the basement for the Springerle molds—which would eventually be found, of course, upstairs in the the far reaches of the kitchen closet. Mother also had an abiding passion for Florentines, with their chewy, crunchy sweetness. And then there'd be things like the traditional sugar cookies cut into Christmas-tree shapes with red and green sprinkles on them.

There was never any great ceremony attached to cookies. They were just set out for us to eat, always, everywhere. As long as we didn't try to wolf them down just before dinner, we were allowed to eat freely of them anytime we wanted. This was Christmas, after all. And if there was one thing the folks understood, it was the concept of party time.

In assembling this collection of holiday goodies, I've tried to balance nostalgia with modern tastes. Since Mother died, I've continued to seek out great old recipes from relatives and longtime family friends. In some cases, I've even substituted more traditional versions of some old German favorites for Mom's variations—as with Lebkuchen and Pfeffernüsse, for instance. At the same time, I've been mindful of the fact that traditions evolve and preferences change. Mother would have said, for instance, that if you don't want to gain weight, just take one cookie; today, we want our cookies low in fat and cholesterol—presumably so that we can have more than one. We have, therefore, added a bunch of reduced-fat recipes here—though I must say that they don't particularly *taste* as if their fat has been reduced (which I mean as a compliment). There's also the matter of techniques and equipment: We know more about the science of baking today than Mother did, and we have access to new kitchen devices and appliances that would have left her wide-eyed. The recipes that follow take this into account.

The other thing I've tried to remember is that each generation develops its own traditions. When my sixteen-year-old son, John, comes home for the holidays, he isn't much interested in Springerle. He wants Candy Bar Bars or Peanut Butter Chocolate Chunk Monsters. He's the one who convinced me that I ought to include Monster cookies here. Mother might have found these "too much of a good thing"; John thinks they're just enough. Maybe one day he'll look back on his Christmases and remember Candy Bar Bars and various Monsters as fondly as I do Mom's Spritz and Florentines.

Ethan Becker
Cincinnati, Ohio
May 1996

COOKIES

Freshly home-baked cookies are one of life's most satisfying pleasures. For most people, the mere mention of cookie baking conjures up images not just of tantalizing aromas and good flavors, but of warm kitchens and good times with family or friends. For many of us it also evokes happy childhood memories of "helping" with the cookie-making process—mixing, rolling-out, decorating, and of course surreptitiously sampling raw dough, chocolate chips, colored sprinkles, and other assorted goodies!

Christmas and cookies are inseparable. Cookies fuel the holiday season even as they help define it. It has always irked us, however, that the enjoyment of these delightful confections should be restricted to a few weeks each year. Some of the recipes that follow are for cookies with a long traditional association with Christmas; others are our own seasonal family favorites, without which we can scarcely imagine the holidays; still others, lots of them, are "anytime" cookies. Our theory is that all of these cookies are special enough for grand occasions—but also perfectly delightful whenever the cookie-making spirit should move us.

Besides the obvious pleasures of the end result, we're convinced that cookie baking is so popular simply because it's so easy, and just plain fun. Cookies usually require only very basic ingredients, equipment, and techniques, and making them truly can be "child's play." On the other hand, as there are definitely secrets to successful cookie baking, we've outlined them here.

MEASURING DRY AND LIQUID INGREDIENTS

With dry ingredients like flour and sugar, the most precise method of measuring is to weigh them on a kitchen scale. This is the first time in *Joy* that we've indicated weights as well as volume in the recipes. In earlier days, home cooks baked more often and had developed instincts for measuring. Now when people occasionally take the time to bake (like at Christmas), they must have precise instructions and results they can rely on. All weights for dry ingredients have been rounded to the nearest ¼ ounce.

If you don't have a kitchen scale (though it seems to us that every frequent baker should), use graduated "dry" measuring cups or spoons in the exact increments called for (1 tablespoon, ½ cup, etc.). Scoop out dry ingredients directly from the container with these cups, then level them by sweeping a long-bladed spatula or knife across the surface; do not pack down. This is known as the "dip and sweep" method of measuring.

For liquid ingredients use clear glass or plastic measuring cups with quantities clearly marked on the sides.

MIXING COOKIES

The method used to mix a dough is directly related to the texture of the finished cookie. Unlike cakes, which can all be made with an electric mixer, cookies range in texture from flaky and crispy to soft and chewy, each

RULES FOR MAKING GREAT COOKIES

◆ The best cookies are made from the best ingredients. Use unsalted butter, and don't stint. If possible, use unsalted nuts, and make sure that they're very fresh. (Nuts are oily, and the oil can turn rancid with age.) Dried fruits such as raisins, dates, and candied citrus bits should always be plump and moist; hard, dried-out "bullets" are not only untoothsome, but will draw off moisture and make cookies dry. Don't economize on baking chocolate or on spices. Believe it or not, there is a dramatic difference between the flavor of genuine cinnamon and that of ground cassia, often sold as a cinnamon substitute. Always buy pure vanilla, almond or other extracts, not imitation which can taste tinny and artificial.

◆ Always use large eggs when baking. Their size is closely regulated for uniformity, one large egg weighing 2 ounces in the shell and 1.75 ounces out of the shell. It is important to note that an egg is a liquid ingredient and substituting extra-large or jumbo eggs will throw off the balance of a recipe.

◆ Baking, unlike some other kinds of cooking, is not a casually improvisational art. Read each recipe all the way through before starting, always preheat the oven for 20 minutes before baking, and measure out all the ingredients carefully before you start mixing them.

◆ A cookie must have certain characteristics to earn it a place in the home-baking hall of fame: a distinctive texture, be it brittle-crisp, chewy-gooey, crunchy, silky or melt-in-the-mouth (great cookies are rarely dry or cakey); an inviting appearance—which is not to say necessarily a picture-perfect one; a size and shape suitable to the cookie's character (oversize and sturdy for munching from a baggy in a lunch box, say, or dainty and chic for perching on a saucer at a tea); and most of all, of course, good flavor.

dependent upon the appropriate mixing technique. We use a variety of methods throughout this book, from the food processor to the electric mixer to beating the ingredients with a spoon. For best results, follow the instructions in each recipe.

TEMPERATURE OF INGREDIENTS: Unless otherwise specified, it's best to let butter, flour, eggs, nuts, and other ingredients that have been refrigerated (or stored in a cold pantry) warm up almost to room temperature before using. If a recipe calls for "softened" butter—and many of them do—make sure it's not too cold and firm (which will make it too stiff and lumpy to fluff up or "cream" properly) or nearly melted (which will make it too thin to fluff up at all). If the butter is too cold or too warm, it can even change the temperature of the dough enough to significantly alter baking time. If possible, let butter soften naturally at room temperature; if you're in a hurry, place it in a microwave-safe bowl and microwave it on low power, checking its consistency every 30 seconds and stirring it lightly when it begins to soften. If no microwave is available, put it in a metal bowl set inside a larger, shallow bowl of warm water and stir frequently as it begins to soften.

SUBSTITUTIONS FOR BUTTER: Some cooks prefer margarine to butter, either for reasons of economy or health. We love butter, and would rather have one cookie made with it than two or three without—but we must admit that with many kinds of cookies, quite satisfactory results may be obtained by replacing up to half the butter with the same amount of regular nondiet stick margarine. (Please do not use diet stick margarine or any tub margarine or "spread" in place of butter, as these can drastically change the texture of the dough.) We cannot in good conscience recommend substituting even some margarine for butter in shortbreads or butter cookies, though, because the flavor of these depends so much on a truly buttery richness.

FLOURS: Although we use all-purpose white flour in nearly all our cookie recipes, we know that some cooks like to incorporate whole wheat flour into their cookies. If you wish to experiment, we recommend that you start with highly flavored cookies (those with molasses or chocolate, for instance), and replace no more than a third of the white flour with whole wheat. If you can find it, whole wheat pastry flour is best. However, cookies made even with this whole wheat flour will always be slightly darker and heavier than the white-flour variety. Once you add flour to the liquid ingredients in a recipe, don't overbeat the dough; this can result in tough cookies, especially in lower-fat recipes.

HANDLING AND SHAPING COOKIES

Resist the temptation to add extra flour to make a cookie dough more manageable during shaping or rolling, as you might if you were making bread or pasta. To prevent most cookie doughs from sticking to your work surface and rolling pin, roll portions between sheets of wax paper, occasionally checking the underside of the paper and smoothing any creases (see illustrations, p. 53). Then keeping the wax paper attached, layer the dough on trays and chill until slightly firm. Molasses doughs are too sticky to be rolled between wax paper, but letting them rest at room temperature for several hours before rolling out tames them enough that you'll be able to get by with minimal added flour. With short, rich doughs that seem too soft to handle, on the other hand, just the right amount of chilling will bring them under control. Refrigerate them until they're firm enough to hold their shape, but remove them before they become too cold and stiff. For doughs that warm up and soften very rapidly, start with only a portion of the dough, keeping the rest refrigerated until needed.

When cutting or otherwise shaping cookies, try to keep them all about the same size and thickness, so that they bake evenly. And remember that if you choose to make cookies larger or smaller than the recipe specifies, the amount of spreading, the baking time, and the recipe yield will vary.

BAKING COOKIES AT HIGH ALTITUDES

Baking, being a delicate process, can be affected by altitude. In general, up to 3,000 feet no adjustments are necessary to obtain attractive, properly textured cookies—and even at higher altitudes, cookies are nowhere near as susceptible to problems as cakes are. It is worth remembering, though, that at high altitudes liquids boil faster, which causes moisture to evaporate quickly (and thus concentrates the flavors of the other ingredients); and that chocolate chip and other drop cookies tend to bake flatter than usual, and are perhaps sweeter. When baking above 3,000 feet, some cooks, and we are among them, recommend that you lower the oven temperature about 25°F, which helps the cookies retain moisture. It also helps to reduce the sugar in the recipe by 2 tablespoons for every 1 cup. For rich chocolaty or very sweet doughs, slightly reducing the baking powder may be helpful. Above 5,000 feet, it is sometimes necessary to reduce baking powder by half and sugar by about 2 tablespoons for every cup. In sour cream doughs, baking soda should not be reduced beyond ½ teaspoon for each cup of sour cream.

DECORATING COOKIES

Decorations greatly assist the appearance (and disappearance) of cookies—but make sure the decorations are suitable. Coarsely chopped nuts or chocolate morsels are wonderful toppings for big, flavorful, rough-textured cookies, but would be out of place on delicate wafers and crisps. Likewise, fine piping, tiny nonpareils, crystal sugar, or dainty dabs of jam are fine for tea cookies, but would seem fussy on hefty drop cookies and bars. We've always liked the idea of decorations that provide a clue to a cookie's flavor: a sprinkling of cinnamon-sugar to advertise a hint of spices; a few coconut shreds to signal a coconut filling; a drizzle of yellow-tinted icing hinting at the tang of lemon zest inside. Somehow, our appetites are heightened by having an idea of what to expect.

To ensure that nonpareils and other garnishes will stay on top of cookies, press them firmly into the dough before baking (use a wide-bladed spatula if the cookies are flat)—or secure them with Royal Icing, p. 108. Cookies can also be decorated with food-coloring paint. To paint cookies before baking, beat together an egg yolk with about ¼ teaspoon water and a drop of the desired food coloring. (Remember that blue coloring will turn green when mixed with the yellow yolk; for a true blue, use egg white instead.) For paint to be applied after baking, simply combine a drop of food coloring with a bit of water to dilute it to the appropriate intensity. (This color wash only shows up well on Springerle, sugar cookies, and other light-colored cookies.) Apply the paint in either case with a soft, fine-tipped paintbrush—or a small pastry brush if detail isn't important.

Don't overdo it, though. A good general rule is to keep cookie decorations simple—unless of course you're baking for (and/or with) children, in which case the more excessively and fancifully decorated the cookies are, the better!

REDUCED-FAT COOKIES

We've always believed that the "rules" of what is now considered healthy eating ought to be suspended when it comes to cookies, especially when they're baked for holidays or other special occasions. Just this once, we tell ourselves, we'll be free with the butter or shortening, not worry about the sugar, add eggs without fear. Nonetheless, we are not unaware of the dietary concerns that face modern man and woman, and we readily understand the appeal of good-tasting cookies made without the traditional abundance of fat, calories and cholesterol. Thus, we have included a number of trimmed-down recipes here.

THE ROLE OF BUTTER: Because some fat is essential for flavor, tenderness, proper crisping, and browning in almost every kind of cookie we can think of (meringue kisses are a rare exception), we've significantly reduced fat without eliminating it entirely. Cookies that might originally have contained 4 to 8 grams of fat apiece, for instance, now contain 1½ to

3½—enough to maintain good flavor and an attractive texture. We've also de-emphasized butter in favor of canola and corn oil. Some butter is usually needed to produce a manageable consistency and a hint of buttery taste, however, so we've left in a little bit.

BUTTER SUBSTITUTES: Please don't be tempted to substitute low-fat margarine or "spread" for butter, since these products tend to have a high water content, which can turn cookie dough runny and yield a flattened-out and overdone end result. If you insist on avoiding butter, use regular nondiet stick margarine instead. You'll lose some flavor, but at least the consistency should be right. Wherever possible, our reduced-fat recipes also cut down on the number of egg yolks used. If a recipe does call for egg yolks, though, it's because they're essential for tenderness or flavor.

It is particularly important not to overbeat reduced-fat cookies, as this can turn lean doughs tough. Pay close attention to recommended baking times, too, and remove cookies from the oven the instant they're done, as lower fat means less moisture and these cookies can dry out quickly.

ABOUT COOKIE MIXES

We know that busy people think mixes and store-bought refrigerator doughs save time. We also know homemade cookies can be made equally fast and taste and look so much better that we cannot, for an instant, recommend these purchased mixes. You need only read the ingredient statements to know that you are paying for ingredients that you would never dream of putting in your family's food. Fresh ingredients and preservatives notwithstanding, anyone accustomed to the texture and pure flavors in even the simplest homemade cookies will immediately taste the additives and exaggerated artificial flavors and find the texture of commercial mixes and doughs unnatural and unsatisfying. If you and your family are used to commercial mixes and doughs, you'll find home-baked cookies a revelation and reward. To our minds, the matchless flavor of real home-baked cookies more than compensates for the extra five or ten minutes spent making them. Start by mastering a few simple bar cookies and you'll soon venture even further.

BAKING COOKIES

PREHEATING THE OVEN: Always turn the oven on 20 minutes before baking.

PANS: Use medium- to heavy-gauge, shiny metal cookie sheets, rimless or with very narrow rims—the kind designed specifically for cookies—so that heat

Rimless cookie sheet

can circulate over the cookies evenly. (A pan with high sides will both deflect the heat and make the cookies hard to remove when baked.) Such sheets come in many sizes, but for most standard ovens, sheets in the 14 x 17-inch range that can accommodate 12 to 16

Rimless cookie sheet with air-cushion inset

medium-size cookies are about right. Dark sheets may cause overbrowning or burning. If cookies burn on the bottom in your oven even with shiny sheets, you may want to invest in very heavy-gauge pans, or ones with an air-cushion inset.

For a more economical approach, try double panning—baking with one sheet set on top of another. Also consider buying an oven thermometer to make sure the stove setting and the interior temperature agree; it is surprising how many ovens are off, in one direction or the other, by 30 or 40 degrees!

If you don't have cookie sheets, create a rimless surface by inverting baking sheets. In the case of bar cookies, if you don't have the baking pan size called for, reduce the baking area of a rectangular pan by folding a piece of foil, inserting it in the pan, and placing dry beans or rice on one side as illustrated below.

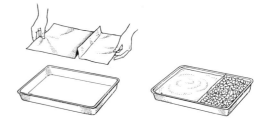

PREPARING PANS: Unless a recipe gives other instructions, always grease baking sheets with butter or shortening or coat with nonstick spray. Several varieties of cookies—for instance, shortbreads and other kinds that contain no eggs but have a high percentage of fat—

can be baked on ungreased sheets. And a few, like meringue kisses and others with a large proportion of egg whites and little or no fat, will stick tenaciously unless baked on parchment paper or generously greased and floured cookie sheets.

Unless your oven is extra large and the cookie sheets extra small, bake only one sheet of cookies at a time—and if you do bake more than one sheet at once, make sure the sheets are the same kind. Don't bake partial sheets of cookies, and be sure not to leave large gaps between cookies; doing either may affect spreading, browning, crisping, and/or overall baking time. If there is only enough dough left for a few cookies, switch to a very small baking sheet, 12-inch pizza pan, or an inverted metal pie tin, so the cookies can be spaced the required distance apart. This will ensure that the heat from the pan is absorbed evenly and that the amount of dough is right for the baking surface. Also, when a recipe specifies baking in the upper, middle, or lower third of the oven, be sure to follow instructions.

TIMING: Many factors can affect baking time, so a range of suggested times is given in the recipes that follow. Always set your kitchen timer to the minimum time specified; it's easy to reset it and bake longer if necessary, but once a pan is forgotten and cookies are overbaked or burned, there is no remedy.

COOLING: When cookies are done, remove the cookie sheet from the oven immediately. As soon as the cookies can be moved without crumbling or tearing, gently lift them one at a time with a wide, fine-bladed spatula and place them flat on wire racks until thoroughly cool. Usually this will be in a minute or two, but it's a good idea to check by trying to lift a test cookie with a spatula every 30 seconds or so. Very tender, short cookies may require considerable standing time, while thin, brittle ones may need almost none. (Where it's necessary to work very fast, we've noted this right in the recipe.) In any case, it is important not to dally when the cookies are ready, as they will continue to bake until removed from the cookie sheet and some may become rigid and stuck. Whenever cookies have inadvertently cooled and hardened, instead of prying them up and risking breakage, return the baking sheet to the oven a few minutes to soften them again.

Cookie sheets should also be thoroughly cooled between batches to keep the dough from warming too much, which can cause the cookies to flatten and spread and in some cases can even cause the butter in the cookies to melt. To avoid any problems, we like to have a couple of extra cookie sheets on hand and rotate among them.

STORING COOKIES

PACKAGING: With so many plastic storage containers and self-sealing bags available to us, old-fashioned cookie tins or jars are no longer essential for storing cookies. Still, as long as their lids fit tightly, they do the job nicely and have a lot more charm than their plastic counterparts. Never put cookies away, in any kind of container, until they're completely cool. Warm cookies will produce steam, which will cause the entire batch to soften, and eventually to spoil. If cookies have been iced or painted, let the icing or coloring set up and dry completely before storing them.

SEPARATING FLAVORS: It is also recommended that you pack each variety of cookie in a separate container. Otherwise, butter cookies and mild bars will quickly take on the flavors of the spicy, citrusy kinds, and snaps and crisps will go soft from moisture borrowed from the thicker, chunkier selections. For extra-large "monster" cookies and oversize bars, the best solution might be to store them individually in sealed sandwich bags.

FREEZING: Although cookies have a well-deserved reputation for keeping better than other baked desserts, most are truly at their peak of flavor in the first few days. Even with cookies that benefit from some mellowing, like spicy honey or boozy fruitcake varieties, fresh flavors begin to fade after several weeks. And cookies laden with butter and nuts may develop off-flavors as the butter fat and oil in the nuts go stale. Fortunately, most cookie varieties freeze well, staying moist and retaining their just-baked flavor for months if packed in airtight containers. Brownies, chocolate chip and sugar cookies, and thin crispy varieties freeze particularly well. If freezing bar cookies, pack them away uncut—in the pan in which they were baked, if you like—then cut into servings when partially thawed.

Though it is easiest to let cookies thaw at room temperature, if you want to eat them right away, lay them on baking sheets and warm in a preheated 300°F oven for a few minutes. Homemade, or even store-bought, cookies that have gone limp from exposure to humidity can also be rejuvenated and crisped this way. When setting cookies out to thaw, it's best to leave them partially unwrapped so they can breathe and condensation doesn't build up. Loosen the lids of plastic boxes or metal tins and untie and partially open plastic bags. Don't let cookies stand out long if the weather is very humid—the crispy varieties, in particular, may begin to droop.

Good storage practices are always our first recommendation, but cookies that have dried out and hardened can also be refreshed. Slip a piece of apple or dampened paper towel into an open baggy or loosely crumpled piece of aluminum foil. Insert into the container of cookies and close tightly. In a few days the cookies will have softened and the apple or towel should be removed.

PACKAGING COOKIES FOR SHIPPING

Common sense tells us that sturdy cookies, the "good keepers," are the most likely candidates for shipping. The best choices are probably small- and medium-size cookies, at least ¼ inch thick and firm in consistency. Although softer, brownies, blondies, and other bar cookies also usually ship well—with the exception of bars with sticky fillings or icings. (Cut bar cookies into portions and wrap individually in plastic wrap, then pack in airtight containers before shipping.)

More delicate varieties can also be mailed successfully if they're packed carefully in tins or tough plastic boxes with plenty of crumpled wax paper added to keep them from jostling each other. Extremely thin, brittle cookies and tender, crumbly ones do not travel well, nor do cookies with sticky glazes or with moist fillings like jam or buttercream. Chewy-soft or fragile meringue kisses and other egg white cookies are likewise an unwise choice; in fact, they may disintegrate completely if thrown about.

After cookies are placed in durable, rigid containers, they then need to be packed in larger boxes filled with Styrofoam bits, plastic bubble sheets, "popcorn," crumpled newspaper, or other airy filler to cushion the goodies inside from bumps and knocks. As added insurance that the cookies will arrive at their destination unbroken, consider shipping by air.

PACKAGING COOKIES FOR GIFT GIVING

Pretty metal cookie tins, ceramic cookie jars, clear glass storage jars, and decorative wooden boxes all make a gift of home-baked cookies more special. Secure containers with loose lids by tying them up with a beautiful ribbon. If you have a modicum of sewing ability, you can also present cookies in fabric sacks tied with ribbon or fancy twist-ties made with wire ribbon. (Slip a plastic storage bag, cut down to size if necessary, inside the fabric for an airtight liner.) Small, dainty cookies can also be tucked in colored bon-bon papers or mini-cupcake cups in flat candy boxes. Resist the impulse, however, to create a sampler of different varieties. Unlike chocolates, cookies will pick up one another's flavors, so that no one cookie ends up tasting quite right. On the other hand, there's nothing wrong with presenting a sampler of one kind of cookie that has been piped, pressed, or hand-formed into a variety of shapes and decorated in several different ways.

CHRISTMAS COOKIES AS DECORATIONS

To prepare a cookie ornament for hanging, use a toothpick to poke a hole through the uncooked shaped dough. When the cookie is baked, remove the toothpick, wiggling it a bit if necessary to widen the hole. Loop ribbon, colored yarn or string, rick-rack, or even fine braid or lace trim through the hole and tie in a pretty bow. The "snow"-covered gingerbread house on p. 107 also makes a charming decoration for the table or mantelpiece.

ABOUT BAR COOKIES

We suspect that bar cookies were invented by someone who enjoyed the ease of making sheet cakes, but who really had a hankering for cookies! Since these sweets are simply spread in a pan, baked, and cut into serving pieces, the time normally taken up with forming dozens of individual cookies is completely eliminated. Still, there can be a lot of variety in bar cookies. Like other types of cookies, bars can range from soft-cakey to chewy-gooey to crunchy and brittle. They can also be left plain, or they can be topped with nuts, powdered sugar, or icing; and they can be cut into squares, from very small to very large, or sliced into narrow strips.

When making bar cookies, pay close attention to the size of the pan called for in each recipe. Variations will throw off the baking time and may affect the texture as well. If the pan is too large, the dough may dry out and the bars will be too thin. If the pan is too small, the bars may become gummy in the center or more cakey than they should be.

A number of bar recipes call for lining the pan with foil, leaving enough overhang on two opposing sides to use as handles as shown in the illustration above. The easiest way to shape the foil is to turn the pan upside down, then smooth the foil around its contours until the right shape is achieved. Foil not only makes cleaning up easy, but means the cooled slab can be lifted from the pan and transferred to a board for cutting in one fell swoop. For bars pretty enough to set out on a buffet table, use a large, sharp knife, and trim away the dry edges before cutting them, wiping bits of cookie off the knife with a damp paper towel as you work.

Unless otherwise specified in the recipe, all bars can be stored airtight at room temperature for several days, or frozen, uncut, for several months. Let thaw partially before cutting into bars.

BROWNIES COCKAIGNE

16 2¼ x 2¼-inch or 24 2 x 2¼-inch bars

Almost everyone wants to make this classic American confection. We are partial to the following recipe, which has appeared in *Joy of Cooking* since the original 1931

edition—unchanged (except for a slight reduction in butter introduced in the 1943 edition, not for health reasons, back in those innocent days, but because of rationing during World War II!) until now. Here we've doubled the vanilla, yielding a more pronounced chocolate flavor. These are the brownies, we always say, "than which there are no others." We always associate them with Cockaigne—which was both a legendary medieval land of plenty and the name given to our house, also known for its abundance of good things to eat.

Have all ingredients at room temperature.

Preheat the oven to 350°F. Line a 13 x 9-inch baking pan with aluminum foil, allowing it to overhang the two narrow ends of the pan by about 2 inches. Grease the foil or coat with nonstick spray.

In a large saucepan over very low heat, melt:

   4 ounces unsweetened chocolate, very coarsely chopped

   ½ cup (4 ounces) unsalted butter

Stir constantly until the chocolate melts and mixture is smooth. Remove at once from the heat. Set aside and let cool thoroughly. Stir into the cooled chocolate:

   2 cups (14 ounces) sugar

   2 teaspoons vanilla

Add:

   4 large eggs

and mix thoroughly. Gently stir in:

   1 cup (5 ounces) all-purpose flour

   1 cup (4 ounces) chopped walnuts or pecans

When the batter is just evenly mixed, turn out into the pan, spreading to edges. Bake on middle oven rack for 23 to 28 minutes, or until the center of the top is almost firm when tapped and a toothpick inserted in the center comes out clean except at the bottom, which will look a little moist. Transfer the pan to a wire rack and let stand until completely cool.

Using the overhanging foil as handles, lift the brownie to a cutting board. Carefully peel off the foil. Cut into bars.

RASPBERRY BROWNIES COCKAIGNE

24 2 x 2¼-inch bars

Raspberries and chocolate are one of our favorite flavor combinations, and this voluptuous new recipe well deserves the Cockaigne name. If you like cakey brownies, mix the batter in an electric beater. If you prefer fudgy brownies, mix everything by hand with a whisk. Cutting these brownies into bars can be messy, so we chill the cooled slab in the refrigerator for about 1 hour before slicing.

Preheat the oven to 350°F. Line a 13 x 9-inch baking pan with aluminum foil, allowing it to overhang the two narrow ends of the pan by about 2 inches. Grease the foil or coat with nonstick spray.

In a small saucepan over very low heat, melt:

> 12 ounces unsweetened chocolate, coarsely chopped
>
> 1½ cups (12 ounces) unsalted butter

Stir constantly until the chocolate melts. Remove at once from the heat. Using a wire whisk, beat until smooth. Cool to room temperature. In a separate bowl, beat or whisk until well blended:

> 6 large eggs
>
> 3 cups (21 ounces) sugar
>
> 2 teaspoons vanilla

Fold in the cooled chocolate mixture with a wooden spoon or rubber spatula. Sift over, then stir to mix:

> 1½ cups (7.5 ounces) all-purpose flour

When the batter is just mixed, turn out into the pan, spreading to edges. Drop by teaspoonfuls evenly over the top:

> ⅔ cup (7 ounces) raspberry jam

Insert the tip of a knife ½ inch into the batter, then evenly distribute the jam by swirling the knife.

Bake on middle oven rack for 30 to 35 minutes, or until the center of the top is almost firm when lightly tapped and a toothpick inserted in the center comes clean except at the bottom, which will look a little moist. Transfer the pan to a wire rack and let stand until completely cool. Using the overhanging foil as handles, lift the brownie to a cutting board. Carefully peel off the foil. Using a large, sharp knife, cut into bars, wiping bits of brownie off the knife with a damp towel as you work.

CHOCOLATE-GLAZED TOFFEE BARS

24 1 x 2⅔-inch bars

A *Joy* Christmas classic made up of a chewy brown sugar-pecan toffee layer spread over shortbread and topped with chocolate, these sumptuous candy-like bars always disappear so fast they remind us of the old family joke about the Sunday motorist who said, "Nice town we are coming to, wasn't it?"

Lightly grease an 8-inch square baking pan.

Using a wire whisk, thoroughly stir together :

> ⅔ cup (3.25 ounces) all-purpose flour
>
> 1½ tablespoons sugar
>
> ⅛ teaspoon salt

Sprinkle over the flour mixture:

> ¼ cup (2 ounces) unsalted butter, chilled and cut into small pieces

Using pastry blender, knives, or fingertips, cut the butter into the flour until the mixture resembles fine meal. Sprinkle the mixture with:

> 2 teaspoons milk

Lightly stir to mix. Knead until the milk is distributed and the particles begin to hold together. If necessary, add 1 or 2 teaspoons more milk, until the mixture holds together but is not wet. (Alternatively, in a food processor, mix the dry ingredients and butter in on/off pulses until the mixture resembles coarse meal; be careful not to overprocess. A bit at a time, add 2 teaspoons milk and process in on/off pulses until the particles begin to hold together; if necessary, add just enough more milk so mixture holds together but is not wet.)

Firmly press the dough into the pan to form a smooth, even layer. Refrigerate for 15 minutes. Preheat the oven to 350°F.

Bake the chilled dough on middle oven rack for 10 minutes. Set aside to cool slightly.

FOR TOFFEE AND CHOCOLATE LAYERS

Spread in a baking pan and toast in the oven, stirring occasionally, 5 to 8 minutes, until very lightly browned:

> 1½ cups (6 ounces) chopped pecans

Set aside to cool.

Combine in a heavy medium saucepan:

> ⅓ cup (2.75 ounces) unsalted butter
>
> ½ cup (4 ounces) packed light brown sugar
>
> 2 tablespoons clover or other mild honey
>
> 1 tablespoon milk
>
> ⅛ teaspoon salt

Stirring frequently, bring the mixture to a boil over medium heat. Boil the mixture, uncovered, for 3 minutes; remove from the heat. Stir in the toasted pecans and:

> 1 teaspoon vanilla

Spread the mixture evenly over the baked layer. Bake for 17 to 20 minutes, or until the mixture is bubbly, golden brown, and just slightly darker at the edges. Transfer the pan to a wire rack to cool until warm. Sprinkle the top with:

> ¼ cup (1.5 ounces) semisweet chocolate morsels

Let stand several minutes until the chocolate morsels partially melt, then smooth across the surface with a table knife to partially spread the chocolate (surface will not be completely covered with chocolate). Garnish by sprinkling with:

> 2 tablespoons finely chopped pecans

Let the chocolate cool until thickened but still slightly soft, then carefully cut into bars using a sharp knife; let cool thoroughly before lifting the bars from the pan. Retrace cuts to separate bars, if necessary.

PEANUT BUTTER CHOCOLATE BARS

18 3 x 2-inch bars

These lush bar cookies are the "fastest" we know, since they are scarfed up almost more quickly than we can make them.

Preheat the oven to 325°F. Have ready a 13 x 9-inch baking pan.

In a medium heavy saucepan over low heat, melt:

> ½ cup plus 2 tablespoons (5 ounces) unsalted butter

Add and stir until combined:

> 2 cups (7.5 ounces) finely ground chocolate cookie crumbs

With your fingers, press the mixture evenly into the bottom of the pan. Bake on middle oven rack for 15 minutes, until dry. Set aside.

Using an electric mixer, beat together until smooth:

> 1 pound (16 ounces) cream cheese
>
> ⅔ cup (4.75 ounces) sugar

Beat in:

> 2 large eggs

Stir in until mixture is smooth:

> ¾ cup (8 ounces) smooth peanut butter

With a rubber spatula, spread the mixture evenly over the baked crust. Bake on middle oven rack for 10 to 15 minutes, until set. Transfer the pan to a wire rack and let cool to room temperature.

Bring just to a boil:

> ½ cup (4 liquid ounces) heavy cream

Remove from the heat and add:

> 3½ ounces bittersweet or semisweet chocolate, finely chopped

Using a wire whisk, beat until smooth. With a rubber spatula, spread the chocolate mixture evenly over the peanut butter mixture. Refrigerate until firm. Using a large, sharp knife, cut into bars, wiping the knife clean with a damp paper towel as you work.

Store, airtight, in the refrigerator, for 3 days, or freeze for up to 1 month.

PUMPKIN CHEESECAKE BARS

18 3 x 2-inch bars

We'd bet that 99 percent of the pumpkin consumed in America every year gets eaten in the form of pies. Here's another way to enjoy pumpkin that will up the "non-pie" percentage. We think of these as perfect treats at Halloween, either for the kids' parties or for the adults to munch on as they wait for the kids to ring the doorbell. On the other hand, they're pretty good on the Fourth of July, Groundhog Day, and Christmas, too.

Preheat the oven to 350°F. Have ready a 13 x 9-inch baking pan.

Using an electric mixer, beat together until smooth:

    ½ cup (4 ounces) unsalted butter, softened

    ¼ cup (1.75 ounces) sugar

Beat in:

    1 large egg

Sift over, then stir to mix:

    1¼ cups (6.25 ounces) all-purpose flour

With your fingers, press the dough evenly into the bottom of the pan. Bake on middle oven rack for 15 to 20 minutes, just until dough begins to brown. Remove the pan from the oven and set aside. Reduce the oven temperature to 325°F.

Using an electric mixer, beat until smooth:

    1 pound (16 ounces) cream cheese

    ½ cup (3.5 ounces) sugar

Mix in:

    2 large eggs

Stir in until mixture is well combined:

    ½ teaspoon ground ginger

    ½ teaspoon ground cinnamon

    ¾ cup (6 liquid ounces) pumpkin puree

    large pinch salt

Using a rubber spatula, spread the mixture evenly over the baked crust. Bake on middle oven rack for 25 minutes, or until firm. Transfer the pan to a wire rack and let stand until completely cool.

Mix together until smooth:

    ¾ cup (6 liquid ounces) sour cream

    1½ tablespoons sugar

With a rubber spatula, spread the mixture evenly over the pumpkin. In a double boiler, or in a heatproof bowl snugly fit over a saucepan of water or in a microwave on 50 percent power, melt, stirring often:

    1 ounce bittersweet or semisweet chocolate

Using a spoon, drizzle over bars. Refrigerate until the chocolate is set. Cut into bars using a sharp knife. Wipe the blade clean with a damp paper towel between cuts. Store, airtight, in the refrigerator, for 2 to 3 days, or freeze for up to 1 month.

LEMON CURD BARS COCKAIGNE

18 3 x 2-inch bars

Lemon lovers finally win out over chocolate lovers and get a bar of their own. Appearing in *Joy* for the first time, these bars offer a thick square of lemony lemon curd sitting on top of a rich, buttery crust.

Preheat the oven to 325°F. Have ready a 13 x 9-inch baking pan.

In a large bowl, sift together.

>   1½ cups (7.5 ounces) all-purpose flour
>   ½ cup (1.5 ounces) powdered sugar

With a pastry blender, knives, or fingertips, cut in:

>   ¾ cup (6 ounces) chilled unsalted butter

Work in until mixture is the size of small peas. Using your fingers, press the mixture into the bottom of the pan and ¾ inch up the sides. Bake on middle oven rack for 20 to 30 minutes, until golden brown. Remove the pan from the oven and set aside. Reduce the oven temperature to 300°F.

Using a wire whisk, beat until smooth:

>   6 large eggs
>   3 cups (21 ounces) sugar

Add:

>   grated zest of 1 lemon
>   1 cup plus 2 tablespoons (9 liquid ounces) freshly
>   squeezed lemon juice (about 5 lemons)

Sift over, then stir until well combined:

>   ½ cup (2.5 ounces) all-purpose flour

Pour the batter over the baked crust. Bake on middle oven rack for 35 minutes, until set. Transfer the pan to a wire rack and let cool completely before cutting into bars.

Store, airtight, in the refrigerator, for 2 to 3 days, or freeze for up to 1 month.

SCOTTISH SHORTBREAD

24 2⅔-inch bars

In medieval Britain, any pastry that was firm but crumbly and made with lots of fat (be it suet, lard, or butter) was called "short." The Scots became masters of this particular variety of short-dough confection. Mild in flavor but fragrant with butter, this classic is remarkably simple to make. For a slightly sweeter taste, sprinkle 1 or 2 teaspoons of granulated sugar over the top after baking.

Preheat the oven to 300°F. Have ready an 8-inch square baking pan or a rectangular shortbread mold.

Using an electric mixer, beat until light and well blended:

> ⅔ cup (5.25 ounces) unsalted butter, softened
>
> ¼ cup (.75 ounce) powdered sugar
>
> 1½ tablespoons sugar
>
> ¼ teaspoon salt

Sift over the butter mixture:

> 1½ cups (7.5 ounces) all-purpose flour

Gradually stir the flour into the butter mixture, then lightly knead until well blended and smooth. If the dough is too dry to hold together, sprinkle a few drops of water over it, adding only enough to hold particles together and being careful not to overmoisten it. Firmly press the dough into the pan or mold, forming a compact, even layer. If baking in a pan, pierce the dough deeply with a fork all over in a decorative pattern.

Bake on middle oven rack for 45 to 50 minutes, or until the shortbread is faintly tinged with pale gold and just slightly brown at the edges. Transfer the pan to a wire rack and let cool until barely warm. Cut almost through the dough, forming bars. If desired, sprinkle the top with:

> 1 to 2 teaspoons sugar

Let stand until thoroughly cool. Gently retrace the cuts and separate into bars.

NOTE: Some shortbread aficionados substitute rice flour or cornstarch for a portion of the all-purpose flour. Unlike wheat flour, rice flour and cornstarch do not develop gluten, and therefore produce an especially crumbly and tender shortbread. If desired, use ⅓ cup rice flour or cornstarch for an equal amount of all-purpose flour in the above recipe.

PETTICOAT TAILS

12 wedges

This traditional British shortbread may get its name from the fact that it's baked in a round pan and cut into fan-shaped wedges—said to resemble the bell-hoop petticoats worn by ladies of the Royal Court in the 18th century. On the other hand, the name might also derive from the French term *petits gâteaux,* or little cakes.

Preheat the oven to 300°F. Prepare dough as for Scottish Shortbread. Very firmly press the dough into an even layer in an 8- to 8½-inch cake pan or round shortbread mold or fluted tart pan. If using a cake or tart pan, decorate shortbread edge all the way around by pressing in tine marks with the back of a fork. Using a table knife, carefully cut round into quarters. Then cut each quarter into thirds to yield 12 equal wedges. Decorate the surface by deeply piercing with a fork at even intervals. Bake for 45 to 50 minutes, or until shortbread is pale gold and just slightly darker at the edges. Transfer the pan to a wire rack to cool to barely warm. Carefully retrace cuts made in the surface, then let shortbread stand in the pan until completely cool.

CHOCOLATE SHORTBREAD

15 3 x 2½-inch bars

A friend of ours used to make this quick but tasty version of shortbread as a travel snack for her kids when they went off to college—and then mail them some more.

Preheat the oven to 300°F. Have ready a 13 x 9-inch baking pan.

Using an electric mixer, beat until light and well blended:

> 1 cup (8 ounces) unsalted butter, softened
>
> ½ cup (3.5 ounces) superfine sugar

In a double boiler, or in a heatproof bowl snugly fit over a pan of water or in a microwave on 50 percent power, melt, stirring often:

> 2 ounces bittersweet or semisweet chocolate

Remove from the heat and let cool slightly. Sift over the butter mixture:

> 2 cups (10 ounces) all-purpose flour

Add the melted chocolate, then stir until well blended. Using your fingers, press dough into the pan. Bake on middle oven rack for 40 minutes, until top is firm when lightly tapped and a toothpick inserted in the center comes out clean. Transfer the pan to a wire rack and let cool until barely warm. Cut into bars and, using a spatula, transfer the bars to a wire rack to cool completely.

Facing photograph: Petticoat Tails baked in a round shortbread mold.

MOTHER KROLL'S LEBKUCHEN

24 2 x 2-inch bars

These traditional German cookies date back to the early 14th century—to the days when honey, not sugar, was the everyday sweetener. Special guilds of secular Lebkuchen bakers formed in the city of Nuremberg, capital of the spice trade and of local Bavarian honey making. There are at least three different kinds of Lebkuchen, and probably hundreds of recipes for each.

When the old German cooks baked with honey, they insisted that it be a year old. We prefer to make Lebkuchen with fresh honey, and judging by how quickly they vanish, this must work just fine. This butterless Lebkuchen recipe, new for this edition, was given to us by an old family friend, Mildred Kroll, who reports that it's the favorite bar among the men in her family.

Preheat the oven to 400°F. Line a 13 x 9-inch baking pan with aluminum foil, allowing it to overhang the two narrow ends of the pan by about 2 inches. Grease the foil or coat with nonstick spray.

In a large saucepan, boil:

> ⅓ cup (2.75 liquid ounces) honey

Remove from the heat and allow to cool thoroughly. Add:

> ¾ cup (6 ounces) packed light or dark brown sugar
> 1 large egg, beaten
> 1 tablespoon freshly squeezed lemon juice
> 1 teaspoon grated lemon zest

Sift before measuring:

> 2½ cups (12.5 ounces) all-purpose flour

Combine with flour and sift over honey mixture:

> ½ teaspoon soda
> 1 teaspoon cinnamon

> 1 teaspoon ground cloves
> ½ teaspoon allspice
> ½ teaspoon ground nutmeg

In a separate bowl, mix together:

> ⅓ cup (1.5 ounces) chopped blanched almonds
> ⅓ cup (2 ounces) chopped citron

Add to honey mixture and stir until well blended. Using your fingers, press dough into the pan, spreading to edges. Bake on middle oven rack for 18 to 20 minutes, until a toothpick inserted in the center comes out almost clean.

Meanwhile, stir together until smooth:

> 1 cup (3.25 ounces) powdered sugar
> 2 tablespoons freshly squeezed lemon juice
> ¼ teaspoon vanilla

Stir enough water into the mixture to yield a fluid, spreadable consistency. While the bar is still warm, spread the glaze over it. Immediately mark into squares and decorate with:

> candied cherries
> whole blanched almonds

as shown in the illustration below. Transfer the pan to a wire rack and let stand until completely cool and icing is set. Using the overhanging foil as handles, lift the bar to a cutting board. Carefully peel off the foil. Cut into bars.

NOTE: If possible, let the cookies "age" for at least 2 weeks to allow the spices to ripen. Lebkuchen will keep for months in a tightly closed tin, especially if, as our grandmother used to say with a twinkle, "locked up."

CANDY BAR BARS
18 3 x 2-inch bars

We believe in making almost everything from scratch, but there's something about store-bought candy bars we've always loved. Here's a recipe that uses them in a homemade treat. We like to use crunchy toffee bars, which can be chopped up and added as is. But feel free to substitute your favorite kind. If using creamy caramel candy bars, freeze them until hard before chopping.

Preheat the oven to 350°F. Line a 13 x 9-inch baking pan with aluminum foil, allowing it to overhang the two narrow ends of the pan by about 2 inches. Grease the foil or coat with nonstick spray.

Using an electric mixer, beat together until smooth:

> 1 cup plus 2 tablespoons (9 ounces) unsalted butter, softened
> 1½ cups (10.5 ounces) sugar

Beat in:

> 2 large eggs
> ¾ teaspoon vanilla

Sift over, then stir to mix:

> 3 cups (15 ounces) all-purpose flour
> ¾ teaspoon baking soda
> ¼ teaspoon salt

Add and stir to mix:

> 10 ounces candy bars, chopped into ½-inch pieces

Turn out batter into the pan, spreading to edges. Bake on middle oven rack for 25 to 30 minutes, until top is firm when lightly tapped and a toothpick inserted in the center comes out slightly wet. Transfer the pan to a wire rack and let stand until completely cool. Using the overhanging foil as handles, lift the bar to a cutting board. Carefully peel off the foil. Cut into bars.

ROCKY ROAD BARS
18 3 x 2-inch bars

Preheat the oven to 350°F. Prepare a 13 x 9-inch baking pan as for Candy Bar Bars.

In a double boiler, or in a heatproof bowl snugly fit over a saucepan of water or in a microwave on 50 percent power, melt, stirring often:

> 4 ounces unsweetened chocolate

Remove from the heat and, using a wire whisk, beat until smooth. Cool to room temperature.

Using an electric mixer, beat together until smooth:

> ½ cup (4 ounces) unsalted butter, softened
> 1½ cups (10.5 ounces) sugar

Beat in:

> 4 large eggs
> 1 teaspoon vanilla

With a wooden spoon, fold in the cooled chocolate mixture. Sift over, then stir to mix:

> ¾ cups (3.75 ounces) all-purpose flour
> 2 tablespoons unsweetened cocoa
> ⅛ teaspoon salt

In a separate bowl, mix together:

> 1 cup (4 ounces) walnuts or pecans
> 1 cup (6 ounces) semisweet chocolate morsels
> 1 cup (2 ounces) mini marshmallows

Stir all but 1 cup of the nut mixture into the batter until well combined. Turn the mixture into the pan, spreading to edges. Sprinkle the remaining nut mixture over the top. Bake on middle oven rack for 25 minutes, until top is firm when tapped and a toothpick inserted in the center comes out slightly wet. Transfer the pan to a wire rack and let stand until completely cool. Using the overhanging foil as handles, lift the bar to a cutting board. Carefully peel off the foil. Cut into bars.

CONGO BARS
18 3 x 2-inch bars

Preheat the oven to 350°F. Prepare a 13 x 9-inch baking pan as for Candy Bar Bars.

In a large saucepan over low heat, melt:

> 1 cup (8 ounces) unsalted butter

Remove from the heat and stir in:

> 2⅓ cups (18.75 ounces) packed dark brown sugar

Add:

> 4 large eggs
> 1 teaspoon vanilla

Sift over, then stir in:

> 2⅔ cups (13.25 ounces) all-purpose flour
> 2½ teaspoons baking powder

Stir in:

> 2 cups (12 ounces) semisweet chocolate morsels
> 1½ cups (5.25 ounces) walnuts
> ½ cup (1.5 ounces) flaked or shredded sweetened coconut (optional)

When the batter is mixed, turn out into the pan, spreading to edges. Bake on middle oven rack for about 25 minutes, until firm when lightly tapped and a toothpick inserted in the center comes out slightly wet. Transfer the pan to a wire rack and let stand until completely cool. Using the overhanging foil as handles, lift the bar to a cutting board. Carefully peel off the foil. Cut into bars.

MOCHA JAVA CONGO BARS
18 3 x 2-inch bars

Add 4 teaspoons instant espresso granules or powder with the flour.

Facing photograph, left to right: Candy Bar Bars, Rocky Road Bars, and Congo Bars.

SPICED APPLE BARS
18 3 x 2-inch bars

These spice-accented apple bars go wonderfully with rich homemade eggnog!

Preheat the oven to 350°F. Line a 13 x 9-inch baking pan with aluminum foil, allowing it to overhang the two narrow ends of the pan by about 2 inches. Grease the foil or coat with nonstick spray.

In a large saucepan over low heat, melt:

> 1 cup (8 ounces) unsalted butter

Remove from the heat and stir in:

> 1⅓ cups (10.5 ounces) packed dark brown sugar
>
> 1 cup (7 ounces) sugar

Add:

> 4 large eggs
>
> ½ teaspoon vanilla

Stir together with a wire whisk and then add:

> 2⅔ cups (13.25 ounces) all-purpose flour
>
> 2½ teaspoons baking powder
>
> 1 teaspoon ground cinnamon
>
> ½ teaspoon ground ginger

Stir in:

> 2½ cups (10 ounces) coarsely grated peeled apple (about 5 medium)
>
> 1½ cups (7.75 ounces) golden raisins

Turn out into the pan, spreading to edges. Bake on middle oven rack for 30 to 35 minutes, until firm and a toothpick inserted in the center comes out slightly wet. Transfer the pan to a wire rack and let stand until thoroughly cool. Using the overhanging foil as handles, lift the bar to a cutting board. Carefully peel off the foil. Cut into bars.

EGGNOG

In an earlier time, we warned against the excessive consumption of raw egg whites by children and invalids, because studies had shown that overproportionate quantities of them could induce biotin deficiency. Today, it has regrettably become necessary to warn that raw eggs, whites and yolks alike, have been shown to occasionally carry the salmonella bacteria, a common cause of unpleasant and sometimes lethal food poisoning. In fact, the chances of contracting salmonella poisoning from uncooked eggs are statistically quite small, especially when you are certain to buy only refrigerated eggs and get them into your own refrigerator quickly. Nonetheless, common sense suggests that it is inadvisable for those who are pregnant, elderly, very young, or immune-compromised to consume food or drink in which raw eggs are an ingredient. Others must decide for themselves whether the enjoyment of old-fashioned eggnog outweighs the slight risk involved.

I. UNCOOKED EGGNOG
20 servings

Rich and extravagant.

Beat separately until light in color:

> 12 large egg yolks

Beat in gradually:

> 1 pound (16 ounces) powdered sugar

Add very slowly, beating constantly:

> 2 cups (16 liquid ounces) dark rum, brandy, bourbon, or rye

Let stand, covered, for 1 hour. Add, beating constantly:

> 2 to 4 cups (16 to 32 liquid ounces) chosen liquor
>
> 2 quarts (64 liquid ounces) heavy cream

Refrigerate, covered, for 3 hours. Beat until stiff but not dry:

> 12 large egg whites

Fold them lightly into the other ingredients. Serve the eggnog sprinkled with:

> Freshly grated nutmeg

II. COOKED EGGNOG
16 to 20 servings

Lightly cooking this eggnog kills any possibly dangerous bacteria in the eggs. Two tablespoons of vanilla can replace the spirits. Do not double this recipe.

Combine and set aside:

> 1 cup (8 liquid ounces) milk
>
> 1 cup (8 liquid ounces) heavy cream

Whisk just until blended:

> 12 large egg yolks
>
> 1⅓ cups (9.25 ounces) sugar
>
> 1 teaspoon freshly grated nutmeg

Whisk in:

> 2 cups (16 liquid ounces) milk
>
> 2 cups (16 liquid ounces) heavy cream

Transfer mixture to a heavy-bottomed 3- to 4-quart saucepan and place over low heat. Stirring constantly, heat mixture until it becomes a little thicker than heavy cream (about 175°F). Do not overheat, or mixture will curdle. Remove from the heat and immediately stir in reserved milk and cream. Pour through a strainer into a storage container. Chill thoroughly, uncovered, then stir in:

> 1½ cups (12 liquid ounces) brandy, cognac, dark rum, or bourbon

Cover and refrigerate for 3 hours and up to 3 days. Serve sprinkled with:

> freshly grated nutmeg

DREAM BARS (ANGEL BARS)   *12 2⅓ x 2¾-inch bars*
Many a copy of *Joy* has been sold on the strength of this recipe. Have all ingredients at room temperature (68°F to 70°F).
Preheat the oven to 350°F. Line a 7 x 11-inch or similar 2-quart rectangular baking pan with aluminum foil, allowing it to overhang the two narrow ends of the pan by about 2 inches.
Using an electric mixer, beat together:

   ¼ cup (2 ounces) unsalted butter, softened
   2 tablespoons sugar
   1 large egg yolk
   ¼ teaspoon vanilla

Stir in, then knead until smoothly incorporated:

   ¾ cup (3.75 ounces) all-purpose flour

Firmly press the dough into the pan to form a smooth, even layer. Bake for 10 minutes; set aside.
Spread in a baking pan and toast in the oven, stirring occasionally, 7 to 10 minutes, or until coconut is very lightly browned:

   1½ cups (6 ounces) chopped pecans or walnuts
   1 cup (3.25 ounces) flaked or shredded sweetened
   coconut

 Set aside.
Meanwhile, beat together until well blended:

   2 large eggs
   1 cup (8 ounces) packed light brown sugar
   1½ tablespoons all-purpose flour
   ¼ teaspoon baking powder
   ⅛ teaspoon salt
   1½ teaspoons vanilla

Stir the coconut-nut mixture into the egg mixture. Spread the mixture evenly over the dough. Bake on middle oven rack for 20 to 25 minutes, or until the top is firm and golden brown and a toothpick inserted in the center comes out slightly wet. Transfer the pan to a wire rack to cool to warm. While the bars are warm, mix together the icing:

   2 tablespoons (1 ounce) unsalted butter
   ⅔ cup (2 ounces) powdered sugar

   2 teaspoons freshly squeezed lemon juice
   ½ teaspoon vanilla

If necessary, stir in enough water to yield a spreadable consistency. Spread the icing evenly over the top. Let stand until thoroughly cool and the icing sets. Using the overhanging foil as handles, lift the bar to a cutting board. Carefully peel off the foil. Cut into bars.

BLONDIES   *12 2 x 2-inch bars*
In an earlier time, these deeply flavorful and chewy bars might have been described as "butterscotch"—a term which seems to have gone out of favor. A blondie, of course, is basically a brownie minus the chocolate.
Preheat the oven to 350°F. Line an 8-inch square baking pan with aluminum foil, allowing it to overhang the two narrow ends of the pan by about 2 inches.
Spread in a baking pan and toast in the oven, stirring occasionally, 5 to 8 minutes, until very lightly browned:

   1 cup (4 ounces) chopped pecans

Set aside to cool. Thoroughly stir together:

   1 cup (5 ounces) all-purpose flour
   ¼ teaspoon baking powder
   ⅛ teaspoon baking soda
   ⅛ teaspoon salt

In a large saucepan, boil, about 4 minutes, stirring constantly, until light golden brown:

   ½ cup (4 ounces) unsalted butter

Remove from the heat and stir in:

   ⅔ cup (5.25 ounces) packed light brown sugar
   ¼ cup (1.75 ounces) sugar

Let cool to barely warm. Then stir in until thoroughly blended:

   1 large egg plus 1 large egg yolk
   1 tablespoon light corn syrup
   1½ teaspoons vanilla

Stir in flour mixture and pecans until evenly blended. Spread the batter in an even layer in the pan.
Bake on middle oven rack for 28 to 33 minutes, or until the top is golden and a toothpick inserted in the thickest part comes out clean. Transfer the pan to a wire rack and let stand until thoroughly cool. Using the overhanging foil as handles, lift the bar to a cutting board. Carefully peel off the foil. Cut into bars.

ABOUT DROP COOKIES

Whoever invented drop cookies, which we used to call drop cakes, deserves a medal. Except for bars, drop cookies are the easiest of all cookies to make, because shaping usually involves nothing more than dropping dough from a spoon. A few call for patting down the dough or spreading it out with the tip of a knife. In most cases, drop cookies are very forgiving: No harm is done if the mixture is slightly stiffer or softer than expected; the results will just be a little flatter or puffier than usual.

Occasionally, however, when the batter must be very fluid, as with Pecan Lace (p. 39), the consistency has to be just right for the desired amount of spreading. When working with this kind of batter, you may want to test bake a cookie or two. If the finished cookie is too thick or has spread too much during baking, stir in a little liquid or flour to thin or stiffen the mixture.

You will notice that we call for dropping dough or batter from a *measuring* teaspoon or tablespoon. This is for the sake of precision and helps ensure that recipe yields and baking times are accurate.

ALMOND MACAROONS

About 2½ dozen 1¾-inch macaroons

Macaroons are Italian in origin, quite possibly from Renaissance Venice. Have all ingredients at room temperature (68°F to 70°F).
Preheat the oven to 350°F. Line cookie sheets with parchment paper or greased aluminum foil.
In a food processor fitted with a steel blade, combine until finely chopped, scraping sides:

> 7 ounces packaged almond paste, cut into small
> pieces
> 1 cup (3 ounces) powdered sugar

Continuing to process, gradually add:

> 3 large egg whites
> ¼ teaspoon almond extract (optional)

Process for 1 minute, until the mixture is smooth.
Transfer the mixture to a heavy saucepan. Cook over medium heat, stirring constantly, until slightly thickened, about 4 minutes. Refrigerate until cooled and slightly firm.
Drop by generous, rounded measuring teaspoonfuls onto sheets, or pull dough off spoon and form into 1-inch balls, spacing about 2 inches apart.

Bake, 2 sheets at a time, in the middle third of the oven for 19 to 24 minutes, or until just tinged with brown but still soft inside. Rotate sheets halfway through baking for even browning. Transfer sheets to wire racks and let stand until the macaroons cool. Carefully peel the cookies from the paper or foil and transfer to wire racks until thoroughly cool.
Store, airtight, for 2 weeks, or freeze for up to 3 months.

AMARETTI (ITALIAN ALMOND COOKIES)

About 4 dozen 2-inch cookies

These delicious little cookies are another kind of almond macaroon—a homemade version of the ones sold wrapped in colored tissue paper and packed in red tins.
Preheat the oven to 300°F. Line cookie sheets with parchment paper or aluminum foil. If using aluminum foil, butter and flour each sheet.
Spread in a baking pan and toast in the oven, stirring frequently, 5 to 8 minutes, until evenly brown:

> 1¾ cups (9 ounces) whole unblanched almonds

Set aside to cool thoroughly. Transfer to a food processor fitted with a steel blade. Add and finely grind:

> 1 cup (7 ounces) sugar
> 2 tablespoons all-purpose flour
> ⅛ teaspoon salt
> pinch freshly ground black pepper

Transfer mixture to a large bowl. Add:

> 4 large egg whites
> 1 teaspoon almond extract
> ½ teaspoon vanilla

Stir a few seconds to combine thoroughly. Drop by measuring teaspoonfuls onto sheets, spacing about 1 inch apart. Bake on middle oven rack 25 minutes for chewy cookies and 30 minutes for crisp ones. Transfer parchment or foil to wire racks. Remove amaretti with a spatula only when thoroughly cool.
Store, airtight, in a cool place, for several weeks, or freeze for up to 3 months.

TUILES (FRENCH ALMOND WAFERS)

2½ to 3 dozen 3-inch wafers

We first encountered these delicate curled wafers in elegant restaurants in Europe, where they are often brought to the table at the end of the meal and served with chocolate truffles, coffee, and brandy. Their name is the French word for tiles, because they are shaped like the curved terra cotta roof tiles so prevalent on the shores of the Mediterranean. Almost paper thin, with a subtle almond flavor, tuiles are curled by being draped, still warm and pliable, over a rolling pin until cool and firm. The hard part is removing them from the baking sheet. All sheets should be clean and cool before each use. The trick is to use a wide spatula with a very thin blade and to work very quickly. Have ingredients at room temperature (68°F to 70°F).

Preheat the oven to 350°F. Very generously grease cookie sheets, or line with parchment paper or well greased aluminum foil. Set out several rolling pins or bottles the same width as the rolling pin to shape the wafers.

Warm over very low heat, stirring, until very soft but not thin and runny:

   5 tablespoons (2.5 ounces) unsalted butter

Set aside.

Using a wire whisk, beat together until very frothy and smooth:

   2 large egg whites
   ⅛ teaspoon salt
   ⅓ cup plus 1 tablespoon (2.75 ounces) sugar
   ¼ teaspoon almond extract
   ¼ teaspoon vanilla

Gradually whisk in:

   ½ cup (1.75 ounces) cake flour (not self-rising),
   sifted then measured

A bit at a time, whisk in the softened butter until the mixture is smooth and well blended.

Drop batter by rounded measuring teaspoonfuls onto sheets, spacing at least 3 inches apart. (Don't crowd, as the wafers spread a great deal during baking.) Using the tip of a table knife and working in a circular motion, spread each portion into a 3-inch round. Very generously sprinkle the rounds with:

   ½ to ⅔ cup (1.5 to 2 ounces) blanched or unblanched
   sliced almonds, coarsely chopped

Bake, 1 sheet at a time, on the upper oven rack for 6 to 9 minutes, until wafers are rimmed with ½ inch of golden brown; rotate sheets halfway through baking for even browning.

Transfer sheets to wire racks and let stand a few seconds. As soon as the wafers can be lifted without tearing, loosen them with a thin-bladed wide spatula and slide them, bottom side down, onto rolling pins.

Leave the wafers on the sheet when removed from the oven, and take them off 1 at a time, so the others remain warm and pliable. If some of the wafers cool too quickly to place on the rolling pins, return the pan to the oven briefly to warm and soften them. As soon as the tuiles are firm, transfer to wire racks until thoroughly cool. Cool, clean off, and grease the sheets or aluminum foil before using again.

Store, airtight, gently nesting wafers one on top of another, with wax paper tucked around them to prevent breaking. They will keep well for 1 week, or freeze for up to 1 month.

PECAN LACE
About 6 dozen 3¼-inch wafers

Lace cookies are a good old-fashioned American favorite. Since much of the appeal of these see-through wafers is in their brittle, caramelized appearance, prepare them on a dry day. Have all ingredients at room temperature (68°F to 70°F).

Preheat the oven to 350°F. Grease cookie sheets, or line with well greased aluminum foil.

Spread in a baking pan and toast in the oven, stirring constantly, 5 to 6 minutes, until very lightly browned:

> ½ cup (2 ounces) **finely chopped pecans**

Set aside to cool. Raise the oven temperature to 375°F.

Bring to a boil in a medium saucepan over medium heat:

> ⅔ cup (5.25 ounces) **unsalted butter**

Adjust the heat and boil butter gently, stirring occasionally, for 3 or 4 minutes, or until the solids on the bottom of the pan turn light brown. Remove the pan from the heat. Add to the butter, stirring to blend well:

> 1 cup (8 ounces) **packed light brown sugar**
>
> ¼ cup **light corn syrup**

> 1 tablespoon **milk**
>
> ¼ teaspoon **salt**

Stir in until well combined:

> 1½ cups (4.75 ounces) **old-fashioned rolled oats**
>
> 2 tablespoons **all-purpose flour**
>
> 2 teaspoons **vanilla**

Stir in the reserved nuts. Drop scant measuring teaspoonfuls of batter onto sheets, spacing 3 inches apart. Do not make the cookies too large, as they spread a great deal. The batter will stiffen as it cools; this is okay. Bake in the upper third of the oven for 6 to 8 minutes, or until cookies are golden brown all over and just slightly darker at the edges. Transfer sheets to wire racks and let stand until the cookies firm up slightly, about 1 minute. Then, using a spatula, gently transfer the cookies to wire racks until cool. If they become too cool and brittle to be removed easily, return them to the oven a minute to soften. Grease the sheets before baking another batch.

Store, airtight, in layers cushioned with wax paper, for 2 weeks, or freeze for up to 2 months.

EASY COCONUT MACAROONS

About 2 dozen 1½-inch cookies

All macaroons used to be based on almonds, but the coconut version has been popular in America for many decades. This old *Joy* recipe, revised for this edition, as well as the two other brand new recipes on this page, are made without flour—a boon to many on special diets.

Preheat the oven to 325°F. Line cookie sheets with parchment paper or well-greased aluminum foil.

Thoroughly stir together until smooth:

> ⅔ cup (5.25 liquid ounces) sweetened condensed milk
>
> 1 large egg white
>
> 1½ teaspoons vanilla
>
> ⅛ teaspoon salt

Stir in until well blended:

> 3½ cups (11.25 ounces) flaked or shredded sweetened coconut

Drop scant measuring tablespoonfuls of dough into 1¼-inch mounds, spacing about 2 inches apart on sheets.

Bake, 1 sheet at a time, in the upper third of the oven for 20 to 25 minutes, or until nicely browned. Transfer sheets to wire racks and let stand until the cookies are thoroughly cool. Carefully peel the cookies from the paper or foil.

Store, airtight, for 3 to 4 days, or freeze for up to 1 month.

COCONUT ALMOND MACAROONS

About 5 dozen 1¾-inch cookies

These smooth, cream-colored cookies feature a crispy meringue-like outside and a moist chewy interior.

Preheat the oven to 350°F. Line cookie sheets with parchment paper or greased aluminum foil.

Beat:

> 4 large egg whites

until they hold soft peaks. Gradually add, a few tablespoons at a time:

> 1⅓ cups (9.25 ounces) sugar

Combine:

> ¾ cup (3.75 ounces) blanched almonds, finely ground
>
> 1 cup (3.25 ounces) shredded sweetened coconut

and gently fold this mixture into the beaten egg whites. Drop by measuring tablespoonfuls onto sheets, spacing about 2 inches apart. Bake, 1 sheet at a time, on middle oven rack for 20 minutes, or until lightly golden. Transfer sheets to wire racks and let stand until the cookies are lukewarm. Carefully peel the cookies from the paper or foil and transfer to wire racks until thoroughly cool.

Store, airtight, for 3 to 4 days, or freeze for up to 1 month.

CHOCOLATE MACAROONS

About 8 dozen 1¼-inch cookies

A dark, crispy, and rugged-looking exterior hides a chewy center packed with coconut, almonds, and chocolate.

Preheat the oven to 350°F. Line cookie sheets with parchment paper or greased aluminum foil.

Combine and set aside:

> 1⅔ cups (8.25 ounces) blanched almonds, finely ground
>
> 2 cups plus 2 tablespoons (7 ounces) shredded sweetened coconut

In a double boiler, or in a heatproof bowl snugly fit over a pan of water or in a microwave oven on 50 percent power, melt, stirring often:

> 3 ounces bittersweet or semisweet chocolate

Cool to room temperature.

Beat:

> 3 large egg whites

until they hold soft peaks. Gradually add, a few tablespoons at a time:

> 1 cup (7 ounces) sugar

Continue beating until the mixture is very stiff and glossy. Fold the nut mixture and the melted chocolate into the beaten egg whites alternately, beginning and ending with the dry ingredients. Drop by measuring teaspoonfuls onto sheets, spacing about 1 inch apart. Bake, 1 sheet at a time, on middle oven rack for 15 minutes, or until lightly browned. Transfer sheets to wire racks and let stand until the cookies are lukewarm. Carefully peel the cookies from the paper or foil and transfer to wire racks until thoroughly cool.

Store, airtight, for 3 to 4 days, or freeze for up to 1 month.

Facing photograph: Easy Coconut Macaroons.

FLORENTINES COCKAIGNE

About 2 dozen cookies

A Rombauer family favorite for years, this recipe may be a bit more complicated than the one in the last *Joy,* but it's worth every new step. These thin, chewy, candy-like Italian cookies are lightly coated on the underside with chocolate. They are always popular, but particularly so with those who like the slightly exotic taste of orange, almonds, and chocolate together. Be careful to prepare the chocolate as directed in the recipe, so that it will set up quickly and stay glossy and smooth.

Preheat the oven to 350°F. Line 2 baking sheets with aluminum foil and lightly brush with 1 tablespoon unflavored vegetable oil.

Combine in a heavy saucepan:

> ¾ cup (5.25 ounces) sugar
> 2 tablespoons honey
> ⅓ cup (2.75 liquid ounces) heavy cream
> ½ cup (4 ounces) unsalted butter, softened and cut into small pieces

Stir over low heat until the sugar is dissolved, about 5 minutes. Raise the heat and bring the mixture to a boil. Brush down the sides of the pan with a damp pastry brush or a damp paper towel to prevent sugar crystallization. Cook the mixture until it reaches the soft-ball stage, 238°F. Remove from the heat and quickly stir in:

> 1¾ cups (7.75 ounces) finely chopped blanched almonds
> ¾ cup (3.75 ounces) finely diced candied orange peel or a mixture of candied orange and lemon peel and dried cherries
> 2 tablespoons all-purpose flour
> finely minced zest of 1 large orange

Drop by measuring tablespoons onto sheets, spacing about 3 inches apart.

Dip the back of a spoon or the tines of a fork into cold water and press the top of each mound to flatten it. Bake for 8 to 10 minutes, or until light golden and set. Rotate sheets halfway through baking for even browning; check frequently to make sure the cookies are thoroughly baked but not overdone. Transfer sheets to wire racks and let stand until the cookies cool. Using a small spatula, gently loosen the confections from the foil.

In the top of a double boiler, or in a heatproof bowl snugly fit over a saucepan of hot water or in a microwave on 50 percent power, melt, stirring often:

> 3.5 ounces bittersweet or semisweet chocolate, very coarsely chopped

Remove from the heat. Add:

> 1.5 ounces bittersweet or semisweet chocolate, cut into ½-ounce pieces

Stir until the melted chocolate cools to just barely warm. Remove any unmelted chocolate chunks. Using a table knife or small, thin spatula, immediately begin spreading a thin layer of chocolate over the underside of each cookie. If the chocolate in the top of the double boiler or bowl starts to set, place it over the bottom of the pan or return it to the microwave for a few seconds and warm just slightly, stirring constantly to blend. Then, continue coating the cookies. Let the cookies stand, chocolate side up, until the coating sets completely, about 45 minutes.

Store, airtight, in a cool place, between layers of wax paper. These will keep well for up to 10 days. Finished Florentines do not freeze well, but the uncoated cookies may be frozen. To finish, thaw to room temperature and then coat with chocolate.

ABOUT MONSTER COOKIES

In recent years, monster cookies—those measuring 4 or 5 inches across—have become the rage. We've even seen them being sold in bake shops in Paris! From a practical standpoint, monster cookies are great labor-savers, since there's much less shaping to do. Large, dense cookies also pack and store well, holding moisture better than small, thin ones. But we suspect that the real appeal of these oversize cookies is emotional: Instead of taking the time to bake a cake, these easy-to-make monsters are grand and festive enough to put a candle in and start a party!

Should you prefer to make regular-size rounds of our monster cookie doughs, we have included alternative shaping directions, baking times, and recipe yields. Always be sure to rotate the cookie sheets halfway through baking to ensure even browning. All six of these cookies, large or small, last 3 to 4 days if stored airtight at room temperature and can be frozen for up to 1 month.

PINENUT MACAROON MONSTERS

15 4-inch or 45 2½-inch cookies

These are as divine tasting as they are beautiful on the plate.

In a food processor fitted with a metal blade, finely grind:

> ½ cup (1.5 ounces) sliced almonds
> 1¾ cups plus 2 tablespoons (13 ounces) sugar

In a separate bowl, whisk until frothy:

> 6 large egg whites

Stir in the ground almond mixture. Add:

> 1½ tablespoons honey
> 1½ teaspoons vanilla

Heat the mixture in the top of a double boiler, stirring frequently, until hot. Remove from the heat and stir in:

> ¾ cup (3.75 ounces) all-purpose flour
> 3¾ cups (20 ounces) pinenuts

Stir until combined. Refrigerate at least 2 hours, stirring occasionally, until cold.

To bake: Preheat the oven to 300°F. Grease cookie sheets, or line with parchment paper or greased aluminum foil.

Using ¼ cup for each monster, drop dough 3 inches apart onto sheets. Bake for 25 to 30 minutes, until golden brown. For regular-size cookies, drop by level measuring teaspoonfuls and bake 12 to 15 minutes. Transfer sheets to wire racks and let stand until cookies cool.

NOTE: Pinenuts are actually edible seeds extracted from the scales of various pinecones. There are two main types of pinenuts: Chinese and Italian. Many people feel that Italian ones, which are longer and thinner, are superior in quality; unfortunately, they're also about twice the price of the shorter, teardrop-shaped Chinese ones. The latter work perfectly well in this recipe—but stay away from those that smell rancid. Pinenuts, with their high oil content, can spoil quickly.

OATMEAL RAISIN MONSTERS

12 4-inch or 50 2½-inch cookies

This is a particularly tasty version of an indispensable classic. Oatmeal cookies are best made with either all granulated or all brown sugar. Granulated sugar will give you crispier cookies, while the molasses in brown sugar yields a moister cookie with a richer flavor. However, we don't recommend using a mix of sugars, as the resulting cookie is much less flavorful.

Preheat the oven to 325°F. Grease cookie sheets, or line with parchment paper or greased aluminum foil.

Using an electric mixer, beat until light:

> 1 cup (8 ounces) unsalted butter, softened
> 1⅓ cups (9.25 ounces) sugar

Stir in, 1 at a time:

> 2 large eggs

Add:

> 1 teaspoon vanilla

Mix in until just combined:

> 2 cups (6.25 ounces) old-fashioned oats
> 2 cups (10 ounces) all-purpose flour
> 1 teaspoon baking soda
> ⅛ teaspoon salt

Add and stir to mix:

> 1⅓ cups (7 ounces) raisins

Using ⅓ cup for each monster, drop dough 3 inches apart onto sheets. Bake on middle oven rack for 20 to 25 minutes, until golden brown. For regular-size cookies, drop by rounded measuring teaspoonfuls and bake 15 minutes. Transfer sheets to wire racks and let stand until cookies cool.

Facing photograph, left to right: Pinenut Macaroon Monsters and Oatmeal Raisin Monsters.

MOCHA WALNUT MONSTERS

14 4½-inch or 50 2½-inch cookies

Preheat the oven to 325°F. Grease cookie sheets, or line with parchment paper or greased aluminum foil. Using an electric mixer, beat until light:

1 cup (8 ounces) unsalted butter, softened
⅔ cup (5.25 ounces) packed dark brown sugar
1½ cups (10.5 ounces) sugar

Beat in, 1 at a time:

2 large eggs

Mix in until just combined:

½ cup (1.5 ounces) unsweetened cocoa
2½ cups (12.5 ounces) all-purpose flour
3 tablespoons instant espresso powder
1 teaspoon baking soda

Add and stir until mixed:

1½ cups (5.25 ounces) walnuts

Using ⅓ cup for each monster, drop dough 3 inches apart onto sheets. Bake on middle oven rack for 20 to 25 minutes, until set around the edges, but still soft in the center. For regular-size cookies, drop by rounded measuring teaspoonfuls and bake 12 to 14 minutes. Transfer sheets to wire racks to cool.

PEANUT BUTTER CHOCOLATE CHUNK MONSTERS

16 4-inch or 50 2½-inch cookies

Preheat the oven to 350°F. Grease cookie sheets, or line with parchment paper or greased aluminum foil. Using an electric mixer, beat until light:

14 tablespoons (7 ounces) unsalted butter, softened
2 cups (14 ounces) sugar
½ cup (4 ounces) packed dark brown sugar

Beat in, 1 at a time:

3 large eggs

Mix in:

1½ cups (16 ounces) creamy peanut butter
¾ teaspoon vanilla

Stir in until just combined:

2¼ cups (11.25 ounces) all-purpose flour
¾ teaspoon baking soda
¼ teaspoon salt

Add and stir until mixed:

1 cup (5 ounces) coarsely chopped bittersweet or semisweet chocolate
¾ cup (4 ounces) unsalted shelled peanuts

Using ⅓ cup for each monster, drop dough 3 inches apart onto sheets. Bake on middle oven rack for 20 to 25 minutes, until golden brown. For regular-size cookies, drop by rounded measuring teaspoonfuls and bake 20 minutes. Transfer sheets to wire racks to cool.

CHOCOLATE PECAN MONSTERS

14 4-inch or 50 2½-inch cookies

Preheat the oven to 350°F. Grease cookie sheets, or line with parchment paper or greased aluminum foil. Using an electric mixer, beat until light.

1 cup (8 ounces) unsalted butter, softened
⅔ cup (5.25 ounces) packed dark brown sugar
1½ cups (10.5 ounces) sugar

Beat in, 1 at a time:

2 large eggs

Stir in until just combined:

½ cup (1.5 ounces) unsweetened cocoa
2½ cups (12.5 ounces) all-purpose flour
1 teaspoon baking soda
⅛ teaspoon salt

Add and stir until mixed :

⅔ cup (4 ounces) semisweet chocolate morsels
1 cup (4 ounces) pecan halves

Using ⅓ cup for each monster, drop dough 3 inches apart onto sheets. Bake on middle oven rack for 20 to 25 minutes, until set. For regular-size cookies, drop by rounded measuring teaspoonfuls and bake 10 to 12 minutes. Transfer sheets to wire racks to cool.

WHITE CHOCOLATE MACADAMIA MONSTERS

14 4½-inch or 40 3-inch cookies

Preheat the oven to 325°F. Grease cookie sheets, or line with parchment paper or greased aluminum foil. Using an electric mixer, beat until light:

1¼ cups (10 ounces) unsalted butter, softened
1⅓ cups (9.25 ounces) sugar
⅔ cup (5.25 ounces) packed dark brown sugar

Beat in, 1 at a time:

2 large eggs

Stir in:

½ teaspoon vanilla

Mix in until just combined:

2½ cups (12.5 ounces) all-purpose flour
1 teaspoon baking soda
⅛ teaspoon salt

Add and stir until mixed:

1 cup (4 ounces) macadamia nuts
1 cup (5 ounces) coarsely chopped white chocolate

Using ⅓ cup for each monster, drop dough 3 inches apart onto sheets. Bake on middle oven rack for 20 to 25 minutes, until golden brown. For regular-size cookies, drop by rounded measuring teaspoonfuls and bake 15 to 17 minutes. Transfer sheets to wire racks to cool.

Monsters, clockwise from top left: Mocha Walnut, Peanut Butter Chocolate Chunk, Chocolate Pecan, White Chocolate Macadamia.

MERINGUE NUT KISSES (REDUCED FAT)

About 3 dozen 1½-inch cookies

Although we advised against putting two cookie sheets in the oven at once, meringues bake in a very low oven and brown only slightly—so in this case, you can bake 2 sheets at the same time. Because the only fat in these cookies comes from the nuts, they end up with less than 1 gram of fat per cookie. Have all ingredients at room temperature (68°F to 70°F).

Preheat the oven to 250°F. Line cookie sheets with parchment or wax paper. If using wax paper, coat with nonstick spray.

In a grease-free bowl with mixer on low speed, whip until foamy:

> 4 large eggs whites
> ⅛ teaspoon salt
> ⅛ teaspoon lemon juice

Gradually raise the speed to high and beat until the whites are frothy and just start to form soft peaks. Then gradually beat in:

> 1 cup (7 ounces) sugar

Beat until the sugar is incorporated, scraping down the sides of the bowl several times. Lower the speed and beat in:

> 2 teaspoons vanilla
> ½ teaspoon almond extract (omit if pecans are used)

Beat several minutes longer, or until the mixture is glossy and stands in very stiff peaks. By hand, fold in:

> ½ cup (2.25 ounces) finely chopped pecans, almonds, or skinned hazelnuts

Using a heaping measuring teaspoonful for each cookie, drop batter into peaked mounds, spacing about 1½ inches apart on sheets. (Alternatively, pipe the batter into 1¼-inch kisses using a pastry bag fitted with a ½-inch-diameter open star tip.)

Bake on middle oven rack for 18 minutes. Rotate pans and switch racks. Bake 18 minutes longer. Turn the heat off and let the cookies stand in the oven 30 minutes longer. With cookies still attached to the paper, place on a flat surface until thoroughly cool. Gently peel cookies from paper.

Store, airtight, for 1 week, or freeze for up to 2 months.

GRAM MENCKE'S FUDGE DROPS

About 3 dozen 2½-inch cookies

These cookies were recently given to us by an old family friend who used to cook 20 or 25 varieties of cookies at a time when she got going for the holidays. She remembers that her mother made them, back in the 1920s—so these are no Johnny-come-latelys.

Using an electric mixer, beat until very light:

> 2 large eggs

Sift together over eggs and stir to mix:

> 1 cup (7 ounces) sugar
> ⅔ cup (3.25 ounces) all-purpose flour
> 1 teaspoon cinnamon
> 1 teaspoon baking powder
> ¼ teaspoon salt

In a double boiler, or in a heatproof bowl snugly fit over a saucepan of water or in a microwave on 50 percent power, melt, stirring often:

> 2 ounces bittersweet or semisweet chocolate

Remove from the heat and add to egg mixture with:

> 1 teaspoon vanilla
> 1 cup (4.25 ounces) chopped walnuts

Stir until evenly combined. Chill dough, covered, at least 1 hour.

To bake: Preheat the oven to 350°F. Line cookie sheets with parchment paper or greased aluminum foil.

Drop dough by rounded measuring teaspoonfuls onto sheets, spacing about 2 inches apart. Bake on middle oven rack for 10 to 12 minutes. Transfer the cookies to wire racks and let cool.

Store, airtight, for 3 days, or freeze for up to 1 month.

ABOUT ROLLED COOKIES

Rolling out cookies may take time, but we love the chance it gives us to play with so many different and exciting shapes and decorations. Sugar cookies and gingerbread men are the best-known rolled varieties, but a number of ethnic and regional specialties, like Sablés (p. 55) and Moravian Molasses Thins (p. 49), are shaped by this method, too.

Rolled cookies are usually cut into shapes with cookie cutters. These can be fun to collect, and an interesting assortment of cutters makes it possible to turn out eye-catching cookies with no extra effort. The rim of a drinking glass or cup may be used if necessary, but it won't provide the variety of shapes or give the sharp, clean edges good tin cutters do. A compromise is to cut the rolled-out dough into diamonds, squares, triangles, or other geometric shapes with a sharp knife.

You can also create your own shapes (tree, bell, rocking horse, etc.) using the patterns illustrated throughout this section. Trace each figure on a separate piece of paper, then enlarge the image on a photocopier. Cut out the shape, paste it to a sturdy piece of cardboard, and cut out the template. To use the template, oil or grease one side lightly, then lay it gently, oiled or greased side down, on a portion of the rolled-out dough. Working carefully, cut around the template with a small, sharp paring knife, then peel off the template and lift out the shaped dough.

To turn out first-rate rolled cookies, the dough needs to be firm and manageable enough to roll and cut out easily. Avoid overflouring or overworking the dough, though; inexperienced bakers often ruin rolled cookies by using too much flour in the rolling process. See "Handling and Shaping Cookies," p. 10.

MORAVIAN MOLASSES THINS

5½ to 7 dozen 2½-inch cookies

These gingery, paper-thin cookies are traditional in American communities settled by Moravian religious immigrants from central Europe. This recipe—an adaptation of one from Old Salem, North Carolina—has been been modified to provide the option of substituting vegetable shortening, now easier to find than fresh lard, and appealing to the vegan.

Using a wire whisk, thoroughly stir together:

   1 cup (5 ounces) all-purpose flour
   1½ teaspoons ground cinnamon
   1 teaspoon ground ginger
   ½ teaspoon ground cloves
   ¼ teaspoon ground cardamom
   ½ teaspoon baking soda

Using an electric mixer, gradually beat together until well blended and smooth:

   ⅓ cup (2.75 liquid ounces) molasses
   ¼ cup (2 ounces) solid white vegetable shortening or good-quality lard
   ½ cup (4 ounces) packed dark brown sugar
   1 teaspoon vanilla

Gradually stir the flour mixture into the molasses mixture, then knead until evenly incorporated. Continue to knead until very smooth, 3 to 4 minutes. Wrap the dough in plastic wrap. Set aside in a cool spot, but not the refrigerator, at least 6 hours and preferably 12. (The dough can be also be stored for several days, but in this case it should be refrigerated. Let come to room temperature before using.)

To bake: Preheat the oven to 300°F. Grease cookie sheets.

Roll out half the dough as thin as possible on a very lightly floured work surface. The thinner the dough, the more cookies it will yield. Lift the dough frequently and dust the rolling pin as necessary to prevent sticking. Using a 2¼-inch fluted or plain round cutter, cut out cookies. Space the cookies about 1 inch apart on sheets. Roll dough scraps and continue cutting cookies. Repeat with remaining dough.

Bake, 1 sheet at a time, on middle oven rack for 6 to 8 minutes, or until just barely darker at the edges; don't overbake, or the cookies will be bitter. Transfer sheets to wire racks and let stand until the cookies are firm enough to lift. Then, transfer cookies to wire racks to cool thoroughly.

Store in small stacks packed in tightly closed baggies placed in storage containers for 1 month, or freeze for up to 3 months.

NOTE: We always get lots of questions about molasses, which, like sugar, comes in different forms. Light molasses, from the first boiling of concentrated sugar cane juice, is the lightest in color, mildest, and sweetest in variety. Dark molasses, from the second boiling, is darker, stronger, and not as sweet. Blackstrap molasses, from the third and final boiling is very dark, thick, and strong, and not very sweet. It is sometimes sold in health food stores as a home remedy—but is rarely used in baking. Light and dark molasses are sometimes bleached with sulphur dioxide gas, giving the name "sulphured" molasses .

GINGERBREAD PEOPLE (REDUCED FAT)

About 2 dozen 5-inch-tall gingerbread cookies

Gingerbread people are always a favorite, and nobody gobbling them up would ever guess that each one contains only about 3 grams of fat. If you like, make Quick Lemon Icing, below, or Royal Icing (p. 108) to pipe on a festive decoration. Even kids are good at doing this.

Preheat the oven to 375°F. Grease cookie sheets.

Using a wire whisk, thoroughly stir together and set aside:

> 3 cups (15 ounces) all-purpose flour
> 1½ teaspoons baking powder
> ¾ teaspoon baking soda
> ¼ teaspoon salt
> 1 tablespoon ground ginger
> 1¾ teaspoons ground cinnamon
> ¼ teaspoon ground cloves

Using an electric mixer, beat until well blended and creamy:

> ¼ cup plus 2 tablespoons (3 ounces) unsalted butter, softened
> ¾ cup (6 ounces) packed dark brown sugar
> 1 large egg

Beat in until smooth:

> ½ cup (4 liquid ounces) molasses
> 2 teaspoons vanilla
> 1 teaspoon finely grated lemon zest

Gradually beat in about half of the dry ingredients. Using a large wooden spoon, stir in the remainder of the dry ingredients until well mixed. Divide the dough in half. Wrap each half in plastic wrap and let stand at room temperature at least 2 hours and up to 8 hours, or refrigerate up to 3 or 4 days, allowing the dough to return to room temperature before using.

Place 1 portion of the dough on a lightly floured work surface. Very lightly sprinkle flour over the surface of the dough and dust the rolling pin. Roll out the dough a scant ¼ inch thick; run a spatula under the dough, lifting it frequently and adding a bit more flour to the work surface and rolling pin if necessary to prevent sticking. Cut out the cookies using a 4- or 5-inch-tall gingerbread boy or girl cutter. Space the cookies about 1½ inches apart on cookie sheets. Roll dough scraps and continue cutting out cookies. Repeat with remaining dough.

If desired, garnish with:

> raisins and/or cinnamon "red hot" candies for eyes and buttons

Bake, 1 sheet at a time, in the upper third of the oven for 7 to 10 minutes, or until edges of cookies are just barely dark. Transfer sheets to wire racks and let stand several minutes. Then, transfer the cookies to wire racks to cool thoroughly.

QUICK LEMON ICING

Stir together until smooth:

> ¾ cup (2.25 ounces) powdered sugar, measured then sifted if lumpy
> 1 tablespoon freshly squeezed lemon juice
> ¼ teaspoon vanilla
> ⅛ teaspoon light corn syrup

If the icing is too thick to pipe or drizzle, gradually beat in a few drops of water until the desired consistency is reached. Scrape down the sides of the bowl several times.

Spoon out the icing into a piping cone or small piping bag fitted with a plain writing tip. Pipe a decorative trim, such as outlines of mittens, a collar, boots, a belt, etc. Or use Royal Icing (p. 108) as "glue" to attach various candy decorations. Let stand until thoroughly cool and the icing has set completely, about 1 hour longer.

Store, airtight, for 3 weeks, or freeze for up to 2 months.

ICED SUGAR COOKIES   *About 3 dozen 2-inch cookies*

These sugar cookies take well to decorative icing. Choose either Quick Vanilla Icing, below, or Royal Icing (p. 108). If you want to make templates in the shapes of the cookies in the facing photograph, follow the directions on p. 49, tracing the illustrations from p. 55.

Preheat the oven to 375°F. Grease cookie sheets.

Thoroughly stir together:

> 3¼ cups (16.25 ounces) all-purpose flour
> 1½ teaspoons baking powder
> ½ teaspoon salt

Using an electric mixer, beat together until well blended and fluffy:

> 1¼ cups (10 ounces) unsalted butter, softened
> 1 cup (7 ounces) sugar

Add and continue beating until well blended and smooth:

> 1 large egg
> 1 tablespoon milk
> 2½ teaspoons vanilla
> ¼ teaspoon finely grated lemon zest (optional)

Beat the flour mixture into the butter mixture until smooth. Divide the dough in half. Place each half between large sheets of wax paper. Roll out a scant ¼ inch thick, checking the underside of the dough and smoothing any creases. Keeping the wax paper in place, layer the rolled dough on a tray and refrigerate about 30 minutes, or until cold and slightly firm.

Working with 1 portion at a time (leave the other refrigerated), gently peel away and replace 1 sheet of the wax

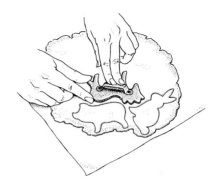

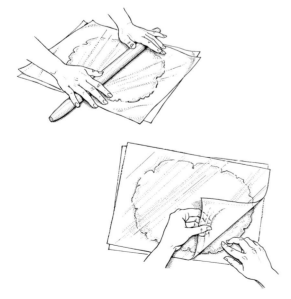

paper. (This will make it easier to lift the cookies from the paper later.) Peel away and discard the second sheet. Using 2- or 3-inch cutters, cut out cookies. With a spatula, carefully transfer them from the wax paper to the baking sheets, about 1½ inches apart. Roll dough scraps and continue cutting out cookies until all the dough is used; if the dough is too warm to handle, refrigerate it again briefly.

If not planning to ice the cookies, decorate with:

> colored sugar or nonpareils

Bake for 6 to 9 minutes, or until just lightly colored on top and slightly darker at edges. Rotate sheets halfway through baking for even browning. Transfer sheets to wire racks and let stand until cookies firm up slightly. Then, transfer the cookies to wire racks to cool.

QUICK VANILLA ICING

Thoroughly stir together:

> 2½ cups (8.25 ounces) powdered sugar, measured then sifted
> ¼ cup (2 liquid ounces) hot water
> 1 teaspoon light corn syrup
> ¼ teaspoon vanilla
> tiny drop of food coloring (optional)

If necessary, add more water to thin or a bit more powdered sugar to thicken until a slightly fluid, spreadable consistency is obtained. If several different colors of icing are desired, divide it among several small bowls before tinting. For more opaque icing, use Royal Icing.

Using a table knife, lightly ice the cookies. If adding nonpareils, sprinkle them on immediately, before the icing sets up. Let the cookies stand several hours until icing sets completely.

Store, airtight, for 2 weeks, or freeze for up to 2 months; pack iced cookies in a single layer.

Facing photograph: Iced Sugar Cookies piped with Royal Icing and painted with diluted colored painting powder, available at specialty baking stores.

SABLÉS   *About 4 dozen 2¼-inch cookies*

Sablés (pronounced sah-BLAY), originally *galettes sablées,* are classic French rolled shortbread cookies, said to have originated in Normandy. Like their American cousins, Pecan Sandies, they are addictive. Cutting the butter into the flour coats the flour with fat, creating the distinctive sandy (*sablé* in French) texture of the cookies.

Preheat the oven to 350°F. Lightly grease cookie sheets. Cut into small chunks:

>   1 cup (8 ounces) unsalted butter, chilled and slightly
>   firm but not hard

Combine the butter in a large bowl with:

>   2¾ cups (13.75 ounces) all-purpose flour

With a pastry blender, knives, or fingertips, cut the butter into the flour to form fine crumbs.

Beat together with a fork until well blended:

>   3 large egg yolks
>   ¾ cup (5.25 ounces) sugar
>   3 tablespoons powdered sugar
>   ⅛ teaspoon salt
>   1½ teaspoons vanilla
>   2 or 3 drops almond extract (optional)

Mix the egg yolk mixture into the flour-butter mixture, then knead to form a smooth dough. Divide the dough in half. Place each half between large sheets of wax paper. Using a rolling pin, roll out each portion ¼ inch thick, checking the underside frequently and smoothing any creases. Keeping the wax paper in place, layer the rolled dough on a tray and freeze about 15 minutes, or until cold and slightly firm.

Working with 1 portion at a time (leave the other in the freezer), gently peel away and replace 1 sheet of the wax paper. (This will make it easier to lift the cookies from the paper later.) Peel away and discard the second sheet. (See illustrations, p. 53.) Using a fluted or plain round 2-inch or slightly larger cutter (or the rim of a juice glass), cut out the cookies. Using a spatula, carefully transfer them from the wax paper to the cookie sheets, spacing about 1 inch apart. Roll any dough scraps between wax paper. Continue cutting out the cookies until all the dough is used; if the dough is too warm to handle at any point, refrigerate it again briefly. Bake, 1 sheet at a time, in the upper third of the oven for 12 or 16 minutes, or until just slightly colored on top and slightly darker at the edges. Rotate sheets halfway through baking for even browning. Transfer sheets to wire racks and let the cookies firm up, 1 to 2 minutes. Then, transfer the cookies to wire racks and let stand until thoroughly cool.

Store, airtight, for 3 weeks, or freeze for up to 1 month.

LEMON SABLÉS   *About 4 dozen 2¼-inch cookies*

Prepare recipe exactly as for Sablés, except *add*:

>   1¼ teaspoons finely grated lemon zest

with the vanilla.

NOTE: The Iced Sugar Cookies illustrated below and in the color photograph on p. 52 may be used as templates for any rolled cookie. Follow the directions on p. 49.

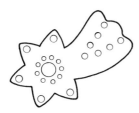

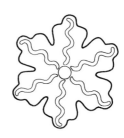

BISCOCHITOS (SOUTHWEST-STYLE ANISE SUGAR COOKIES)

About 3 dozen 2½-inch cookies

A great favorite in New Mexico, these crisp and tender anise-flavored sugar cookies are traditionally made with lard, and we recommend it, since it lends them their special character. If you can't find good-quality fresh lard, solid white vegetable shortening may be substituted.

Preheat the oven to 375°F. Grease cookie sheets.

Thoroughly stir together and set aside:

> 2¼ cups (11.25 ounces) all-purpose flour
> 2 teaspoons ground anise seed, or 1½ teaspoons anise extract (if using extract, add with the citrus zests)
> ½ teaspoon baking powder
> ¼ teaspoon salt

Using an electric mixer, beat until very fluffy and smooth:

> ½ cup (4 ounces) lard or solid white vegetable shortening
> ⅓ cup (2.75 ounces) unsalted butter, softened
> ¾ cup (5.25 ounces) sugar

Add and continue beating until smoothly incorporated:

> 1 large egg plus 1 large yolk
> ¾ teaspoon finely grated lemon zest
> ½ teaspoon finely grated orange zest

Gradually beat the flour mixture into the butter mixture until well blended. Shape the dough into a ball, then divide in half. Place each half between sheets of wax paper. Roll out ⅛ inch thick, checking the underside occasionally and smoothing any creases. Keeping the wax paper in place, layer the rolled dough on a tray and refrigerate for 25 to 30 minutes, or until chilled and slightly firm.

Working with 1 portion at a time (leave the other refrigerated), gently peel away and replace 1 sheet of the wax paper. (This will make it easier to lift the cookies from the paper later.) Peel away and discard the second sheet. (See illustrations, p. 53.) Cut out the cookies using a 2½-inch cutter.

With a spatula, transfer the cookies from the wax paper to the sheets, spacing about 1¼ inches apart. Roll any dough scraps, and continue cutting out cookies until all the dough is used. Chill dough if it becomes too soft to handle. Repeat the rolling and cutting-out process with the second layer of dough. Lightly sprinkle the cookies with:

> 1 teaspoon ground cinnamon mixed with 2½ tablespoons sugar

Bake, 1 sheet at a time, in the upper third of the oven for 7 to 9 minutes, or until just tinged with brown at the edges. Transfer sheets to wire racks and let the cookies firm up slightly. Then, transfer the cookies to wire racks and let stand until thoroughly cool.

Store, airtight, for several weeks, or freeze for up to 2 months.

NOTE: Follow the directions on p. 49 to make templates for the fleur-de-lys and other shapes below.

Facing photograph: Biscochitos cut in the shape of fleurs-de-lys.

RICH ROLLED SUGAR COOKIES

2½ to 3½ dozen 2½- to 3½-inch cookies

Christmas wouldn't be Christmas without an assortment of these. This is the dough just waiting for that collection of cookie cutters you've squirrelled away. If you don't have cutters, make a template by tracing the shapes below on a piece of paper, enlarging them on a photocopier, and pasting them on cardboard (see p. 49). Have fun decorating the different shapes with colored sprinkles or sugar. For a more elaborate finish, pipe with Royal Icing, p. 108.

Preheat the oven to 350°F. Lightly grease cookie sheets. Using an electric mixer, beat until very fluffy and well blended:

    1 cup (8 ounces) unsalted butter, softened
    ⅔ cup (4.75 ounces) sugar

Add and beat in until evenly incorporated:

    1 large egg
    ¼ teaspoon baking powder
    ⅛ teaspoon salt
    1½ teaspoons vanilla

Stir in until well blended and smooth:

    2⅓ cups (11.75 ounces) all-purpose flour

Divide the dough in half and shape into circles. Place each circle between large sheets of wax paper. Roll out a scant ¼ inch thick, checking the underside frequently and smoothing out any creases. Keeping the wax paper in place, layer the rolled dough on a tray and refrigerate for 20 to 30 minutes, or until cold and slightly firm but not hard.

Working with 1 portion of dough (leave the other refrigerated), gently peel away and replace 1 sheet of the wax paper. (This will make it easier to lift the cookies from the paper later.) Peel off and discard the second layer. (See illustrations, p. 53.) Using 2- or 3-inch cutters, cut out cookies. With a wide spatula, carefully transfer them from the wax paper to the cookie sheets, spacing about 1 inch apart. Roll any dough scraps between wax paper and continue cutting out cookies until all the dough is used. If the dough becomes too warm to handle at any point, refrigerate it again briefly. If desired, very lightly sprinkle the cookies with:

    colored sprinkles or colored decorating sugar

Bake, 1 sheet at a time, in the upper third of the oven for 6 to 9 minutes, or until cookies are just slightly colored on top and slightly darker at the edges. Rotate sheets halfway through baking for even browning. Transfer sheets to wire racks and let the cookies firm up, to 1 to 2 minutes. Then, transfer the cookies to wire racks and let stand until thoroughly cool. If desired, decorate with Royal Icing, p. 108.

Store, airtight, for 1 or 2 weeks, or freeze for up to 1 month.

Facing photograph: Rich Rolled Sugar Cookies decorated with piped Royal Icing colored with food coloring paste.

CINNAMON STARS

About 2½ dozen 2½-inch star-shaped cookies

Most rolled doughs are flour-based, but these are made with meringue, resulting in chewy-crisp cookies with an intriguing spice and almond flavor. Cinnamon Stars are a *Joy* Christmastime classic, often packed in our gift tins, but always at the last minute, as they do not keep well. Have all ingredients at room temperature (68°F to 70°F).

Preheat the oven to 275°F. Thoroughly grease and flour cookie sheets or line with parchment paper.

In a completely grease-free bowl with mixer on medium speed, whisk until frothy:

> 3 large egg whites
> ⅛ teaspoon salt

Gradually add:

> 2 cups (6.5 ounces) powdered sugar, measured then sifted

Continue beating until the sugar is fully incorporated and the meringue is shiny and stiff. Remove a generous ½ cup of the meringue mixture, cover, and set aside to use as glaze.

Finely grind and fold into the remaining meringue mixture until evenly incorporated:

> 2½ cups (10.25 ounces) blanched slivered almonds
> 1 tablespoon ground cinnamon
> ¾ teaspoon finely grated lemon zest

Heavily dust the dough with powdered sugar. Gradually knead in enough powdered sugar (about ½ to ⅔ cup, 1.5 to 2 ounces) to make the dough manageable. Set the dough aside to rest a few minutes.

Divide the dough in half and place between sheets of wax paper. Roll out each half a scant ¼ inch thick, occasionally checking the underside and smoothing any creases. Working with 1 portion at a time, gently peel away and replace 1 sheet of the wax paper. (This will make it easier to lift the cookies from the paper later.) Peel away and discard the second sheet. (See illustrations, p. 53.) Using a 2½-inch star-shaped cutter, cut out cookies, dipping the cutter in powdered sugar occasionally to prevent sticking. Using a spatula, transfer the cookies to sheets, spacing about 2 inches apart. Roll dough scraps between wax paper and continue cutting out cookies until all the dough is used.

Gradually stir into the reserved meringue mixture:

> 1 to 2½ teaspoons freshly squeezed lemon juice

Add enough juice to give the glaze a spreadable consistency. Using a table knife, ice the top of each star with a layer of glaze. Add a few extra drops of water to the glaze if it begins to dry out.

Bake, 1 sheet at a time, on middle oven rack for 27 to 32 minutes, until lightly colored and crisp on the outside but still slightly chewy on the inside. Transfer sheets to wire racks and let stand several minutes. Then, immediately transfer the cookies to wire racks and cool thoroughly. Let the cookies mellow a few hours before serving. Store, airtight, for 1 week, or freeze for up to 2 months.

ABOUT HAND-SHAPED COOKIES

Hand-shaping is the art of forming dough into different shapes. It is the method that lends cookies a certain character and personality. Imagine a Christmas tray without Viennese Crescents or sugar-studded pretzels!

It is important to note that the dough should be handled as little as possible. Warm hands can affect the texture of the cookies, especially those with a high butter content. We've illustrated below some of the most common hand-shaping techniques. Many cookies begin as balls of dough which are rolled and then curved into crescents; flattened into rounds with the bottom of a drinking glass, either oiled or dipped into sugar or water to prevent sticking; or pressed down with the tines of a fork, leaving an attractive crisscross pattern in the cookie surface. In the case of biscotti, dough is formed into logs or thin loaves, baked until almost firm, then cut crosswise on the diagonal into individual slices and baked again.

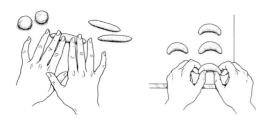

Rolling and shaping crescents

*Flattening balls of dough into rounds
with the bottom of a glass*

*Flattening balls of dough with the
tines of a fork*

CORNMEAL COOKIES   *About 4 dozen 2-inch cookies*

White cornmeal is traditionally used for these rich, sandy-textured cookies, native to the American Southwest and Mexico, because its flavor is considered more delicate—but yellow cornmeal also yields good results. Preheat the oven to 350°F. Grease cookie sheets.

Using an electric mixer, beat together until very fluffy and well blended:

    1 cup (8 ounces) unsalted butter, softened

    ⅔ cup (4.75 ounces) sugar

    2 large egg yolks

    1½ teaspoons vanilla

    ⅛ teaspoon salt

Beat in until thoroughly incorporated:

    ¾ cup (3.5 ounces) white cornmeal

Stir in, then knead until evenly incorporated:

    2 cups (10 ounces) all-purpose flour

Let the dough stand for 5 minutes. Pulling off small pieces of dough, roll between the palms to form scant 1-inch balls. Lightly press 1 side into:

    ¾ cup (4 ounces) pinenuts or slivered almonds

Space the balls, nut side up, about 1 inch apart on sheets. With the palm of your hand, press each ball into a 1¾-inch round. Carefully pat the pinenuts to embed.

Bake, 1 sheet at a time, on middle oven rack for 12 to 16 minutes, or until barely colored on top and lightly browned at the edges. Rotate sheet halfway through baking for even browning. Transfer sheets to wire racks and let stand briefly. Then, transfer the cookies to wire racks and let cool thoroughly.

Store, airtight, for 1 week, or freeze for up to 1 month.

MEXICAN WEDDING CAKES

About 5 dozen 1¼-inch cookies

In Mexico, where they're often served at weddings, these are known as *Pastelitas de Boda,* or Little Wedding Cakes. We call them Pecan Butter Balls, and eat them anytime.

Preheat the oven to 350°F. Grease cookie sheets.

Spread in a baking pan and toast in the oven, stirring occasionally, 5 to 8 minutes, until lightly browned:

> 1 cup (4 ounces) coarsely chopped pecans

Set aside to cool thoroughly. Using a nut grinder, food processor, or blender, grind until very finely chopped but not powdery or oily.

Using an electric mixer, beat until very fluffy and well blended:

> 1 cup (8 ounces) unsalted butter, softened
>
> ¼ teaspoon salt
>
> ½ cup (1.75 ounces) powdered sugar
>
> 2 teaspoons vanilla

Gradually beat the pecans into the butter mixture. Sift over, then beat in until evenly incorporated:

> 2 cups (10 ounces) all-purpose flour

Pull off pieces of the dough and roll between the palms into generous 1-inch balls. Space 1¼ inches apart on sheets.

Bake, 1 sheet at a time, in the upper third of the oven for 12 to 15 minutes, until faintly tinged with brown. Transfer sheets to wire racks and let the cookies firm up slightly. Then, transfer the cookies to wire racks to cool thoroughly. Roll in, until evenly coated:

> ⅓ cup (1 ounce) powdered sugar

Store, airtight, for 2 weeks, or freeze for up to 1 month. If freezing, omit powdered sugar until cookies have thawed.

VIENNESE CRESCENTS

About 4 dozen 2¼-inch cookies

Preheat the oven to 350°F. Grease cookie sheets.

Using an electric mixer, beat until light and creamy:

> 1 cup (8 ounces) unsalted butter

Sift over the butter:

> ¾ cup (3 ounces) powdered sugar

Beat well, then add:

> 2 teaspoons vanilla
>
> 1 cup (4 ounces) ground walnuts or ground blanched almonds

Sift over the butter mixture:

> 2 cups (10 ounces) all-purpose flour

Gradually stir in the flour, then knead until well blended.

Pull off generous 1-tablespoon pieces of dough and shape into crescents (see illustrations, p. 61). (If the dough is soft and hard to handle, refrigerate until firmed up slightly.)

Bake, 1 sheet at a time, in the upper third of the oven for 13 to 16 minutes, or until the crescents are lightly tinged with brown and barely darker at the edges. Transfer sheets to wire racks and let the cookies firm up slightly, about 2 minutes. Then, transfer the cookies to wire racks to cool thoroughly. Sift over, until evenly coated:

> ⅔ cup (2 ounces) powdered sugar

Store, airtight, for 2 weeks, or freeze for up to 1 month. If freezing, omit powdered sugar until cookies have thawed.

KOURAMBIEDES

About 4 dozen 1¼-inch cookies

These Greek cookies are so buttery and fine in texture that they melt in the mouth.

Using an electric mixer, beat until light and creamy:

> 1½ cups (12 ounces) unsalted butter, softened
>
> ¼ teaspoon salt

Beat in until very fluffy and well blended:

> ⅔ cup (2 ounces) powdered sugar
>
> 1 large egg yolk
>
> 2 tablespoons brandy
>
> 1 teaspoon vanilla

Gradually add, beating well:

> 3 cups (15 ounces) all-purpose flour, measured then sifted

Cover and refrigerate the dough for 1 hour, or until firm enough to shape into balls.

To bake: Preheat the oven to 350°F. Lightly grease cookie sheets.

Pull off pieces of the dough and roll between the palms into generous 1-inch balls. Space them 1 inch apart on sheets. If desired, garnish the balls by inserting into the top of each:

> 1 whole clove (about 1 tablespoon total)

Bake, 1 sheet at a time, in the upper third of the oven for 14 to 18 minutes, until just faintly tinged with brown. Transfer sheets to wire racks and let the cookies firm up slightly. Then, gently transfer the cookies to wire racks and let stand until thoroughly cool. Sift over, until evenly coated:

> ½ cup (1.75 ounces) powdered sugar

Store, airtight, for 2 weeks, or freeze for up to 1 month. If freezing, omit powdered sugar until cookies have thawed. Handle gently, as these cookies are fragile.

Facing photograph, top to bottom: Mexican Wedding Cakes, Viennese Crescents, and Kourambiedes.

PFEFFERNÜSSE (PEPPERNUTS)

About 5 dozen 1-inch cookies

Another old-fashioned German favorite especially popular at Christmas, these little cookies get their name from the fact that they're usually small enough to pop into the mouth in one bite, and are pungent with spices—black pepper included!

Using a wire whisk, thoroughly stir together then set aside:

> 1 cup plus 1 tablespoon (5.25 ounces) all-purpose flour
> 1 teaspoon ground cinnamon
> ½ teaspoon ground cardamom
> ¼ teaspoon ground cloves
> ¼ teaspoon ground nutmeg
> ¼ teaspoon baking powder
> ⅛ teaspoon baking soda
> ⅛ teaspoon black pepper
> ⅛ teaspoon salt

Beat until very light and well blended:

> ¼ cup (2 ounces) unsalted butter, softened
> ½ cup (3.5 ounces) sugar

Thoroughly beat in:

> 1 large egg yolk

Add, stirring until evenly incorporated:

> ¼ cup (1 ounce) blanched slivered almonds, finely chopped
> ¼ cup (1.25 ounces) finely chopped candied orange peel
> 1 teaspoon finely grated lemon zest

Stir the flour mixture into the butter mixture in thirds, alternating with:

> 3 tablespoons light or dark molasses
> 3 tablespoons brandy

Cover and refrigerate the dough for at least 8 hours and up to several days, to allow flavors to blend.

To bake: Preheat the oven to 350°F. Grease cookie sheets.

Pull off pieces of the dough and roll between the palms into scant ¾-inch balls. Space about 1 inch apart on sheets.

Bake, 1 sheet at a time, in the upper third of the oven for 12 to 14 minutes, or until cookies are very faintly tinged with brown on top and just slightly darker at the edges. Transfer sheets to wire racks and let cookies stand briefly. Using a spatula, lift the cookies from the sheet and roll until well covered in:

> ½ to ⅔ cup (1.75 to 2 ounces) powdered sugar

Let cool thoroughly.

Store, airtight, for 3 weeks, or freeze for up to 2 months. If freezing, omit the powdered sugar until cookies have thawed.

The cookies may firm up and even become hard during storage. To soften them slightly, add an apple slice wrapped in a paper towel or in an open plastic bag to the storage container. In a few days the cookies will soften, and the apple can be discarded.

BRANDIED FRUITCAKE DROPS
(REDUCED FAT)   *About 3 dozen 1½-inch cookies*

These are spicy, fragrant, and chockablock with dried fruit. Like fruitcake itself, these are good keepers. Thoroughly stir together in a glass or ceramic bowl:

> 1 cup (5 ounces) mixed diced candied citrus peel
> 1 cup (5 ounces) golden raisins
> 1 cup (5 ounces) dried black currants or dark raisins
> ½ cup (2.5 ounces) chopped candied red and green cherries
> ⅓ cup (1.25 ounces) chopped walnuts or pecans
> ½ cup (4 liquid ounces) brandy
> ¼ cup (2 liquid ounces) water
> 1 teaspoon finely grated orange zest

Cover and let stand, stirring several times, at least 8 hours and up to 24.

Using a wire whisk, thoroughly stir together:

> ⅔ cup (3.25 ounces) all-purpose flour
> ¾ teaspoon ground cinnamon
> ½ teaspoon ground ginger
> ¼ teaspoon ground nutmeg
> ¼ teaspoon baking powder

Using an electric mixer, beat together until well blended:

> 3 tablespoons unsalted butter, softened
> 3 tablespoons packed light or dark brown sugar

Add, beating until smoothly incorporated:

> 2 tablespoons light or dark corn syrup
> 2 large egg whites

Stir the dry ingredients and dried fruit mixture into the butter mixture until evenly incorporated. Cover and freeze the dough at least 2 hours, or until firm enough to shape into balls. (The dough may be packed airtight and frozen for up to 2 weeks, if desired.)

To bake: Preheat the oven to 350°F. Coat cookie sheets with nonstick spray.

With lightly oiled hands, roll dough into 1-inch balls between palms. (Wipe off any buildup with paper towels and re-oil hands as necessary.) Space the balls about 1½ inches apart on sheets. Garnish each cookie with:

> 1 candied cherry quarter or other bit of diced candied fruit

Bake, 1 sheet at a time, on middle oven rack for 9 to 12 minutes, or until the cookies are barely firm when gently pressed on top. Transfer sheets to wire racks and let stand, 2 to 3 minutes. Then, transfer the cookies to wire racks and let cool completely. For best flavor, allow the cookies to mellow 24 hours before serving.

Store, airtight, for 4 weeks, or freeze for up to 6 months.

CHOCOLATE CHIP COOKIES COCKAIGNE

About 3 dozen 2½-inch cookies

The definitive classic American cookie, with a twist: finely ground rolled oats, giving them a chewy crunch and a flavor all their own.

Preheat the oven to 375°F. Grease cookie sheets.

Thoroughly stir together:

> 1⅔ cups (8.25 ounces) all-purpose flour
>
> 1¼ teaspoons baking soda
>
> ¾ teaspoon baking powder
>
> ¼ teaspoon salt

Using a electric mixer, beat until light and fluffy:

> 1 cup (8 ounces) unsalted butter, softened

Add, beating until very fluffy and smooth:

> ¾ cup (5.25 ounces) sugar
>
> ⅔ cup (5.25 ounces) packed light brown sugar
>
> 1 large egg
>
> 1½ tablespoons milk
>
> 2½ teaspoons vanilla

Beat the flour mixture into the butter mixture until evenly incorporated. Stir in:

> 1⅓ cups (4 ounces) rolled oats, ground fine in a blender or food processor
>
> 1 cup (6 ounces) semisweet chocolate morsels
>
> 3-ounce milk chocolate bar, coarsely grated or finely chopped
>
> ¾ cup (3 ounces) chopped walnuts or pecans (optional)

With lightly greased hands, shape the dough into generous 1½-inch balls. Space about 2 inches apart on sheets. Pat down the tops of the balls just slightly.

Bake, 1 sheet at a time, in the upper third of the oven for 8 to 12 minutes, or until just tinged with brown. Rotate sheets halfway through baking to ensure even browning; be very careful not to overbake. (Cookies should be still soft in the centers.) Transfer sheets to wire racks and let the cookies firm up, 3 to 4 minutes. Then, transfer the cookies to wire racks until thoroughly cool.

Store, airtight, for 1 week, or freeze for up to 1 month.

OATMEAL CHOCOLATE CHIP COOKIES (REDUCED FAT)

About 3 dozen 2½- to 2¾-inch cookies

We couldn't resist bending our rules a bit here to include a drop cookie in the hand-shaped section, in order to give chocolate chip cookie lovers a lean alternative.

Preheat the oven to 375°F. Coat cookie sheets with nonstick spray.

Using a wire whisk, thoroughly stir together:

> 1¼ cups (6.25 ounces) all-purpose flour
>
> ¾ teaspoon baking soda
>
> ¾ teaspoon baking powder
>
> ¼ teaspoon salt

Beat together until very well blended:

> ¼ cup (2 liquid ounces) corn or canola oil
>
> 2 tablespoons unsalted butter, softened
>
> 1 cup (8 ounces) packed dark brown sugar
>
> 1 large egg plus 1 large egg white
>
> ⅓ cup (2.75 liquid ounces) light or dark corn syrup
>
> 1 tablespoon skim milk
>
> 2½ teaspoons vanilla

Stir into batter:

> 2 cups (5 ounces) old-fashioned rolled oats
>
> 1 cup (6 ounces) reduced-fat semisweet chocolate morsels

Let mixture stand for 10 minutes so oats can absorb some moisture. Stir in flour mixture; dough will be slightly soft. Drop dough by measuring tablespoonfuls onto sheets, spacing about 2½ inches apart.

Bake, 1 sheet at a time, on middle oven rack for 7 to 10 minutes, or until cookies are tinged with brown all over and center tops are just barely firm when lightly pressed; be careful not to overbake. Transfer sheets to wire racks and let cookies firm up slightly, about 2 minutes. Then, transfer cookies to wire racks until thoroughly cool.

Store, airtight, with wax paper between layers, for 3 days, or freeze for up to 3 weeks.

Facing photograph: Chocolate Chip Cookies Cockaigne.

BENNE SEED WAFERS (SESAME SEED WAFERS)

About 4½ dozen 2¼-inch cookies

West African for "sesame," *benne* is still used all over the South—where it is sometimes said that eating sesame seeds brings good luck. Benne Seed Wafers are so nutty-tasting that people often think they contain peanuts.

Preheat the oven to 375°F. Lightly grease cookie sheets. Place in a large skillet over medium heat:

> ¾ cup (4.5 ounces) sesame seeds

Toast the seeds, stirring them or shaking the pan every few seconds, for 5 to 7 minutes, or until they just turn pale brown. Immediately remove from the heat, continuing to stir for 30 seconds. Let cool thoroughly.

Using a wire whisk, thoroughly stir together, then set aside:

> 1½ cups (7.5 ounces) all-purpose flour
> 1¼ teaspoons baking powder
> ½ teaspoon baking soda
> ¼ teaspoon salt

Using an electric mixer, beat together until very fluffy and well blended:

> ½ cup (4 ounces) unsalted butter, softened
> ¾ cup (6 ounces) packed light brown sugar

Add, continuing to beat until well blended:

> 1 large egg
> 1½ teaspoons vanilla

Beat the dry ingredients and ⅓ cup (2 ounces) of the sesame seeds into the butter mixture until evenly incorporated. (The remaining seeds will be used for garnish.)

Pull off pieces of the dough and shape into 1-inch balls. Dip the top of each ball into the remaining sesame seeds to coat. Space the balls, seeded side up, about 2 inches apart on sheets. Gently flatten the balls into 1½-inch rounds with the heel of the hand.

Bake, 1 sheet at a time, on middle oven rack for 6 to 9 minutes, or until the cookies are just lightly browned at the edges. Rotate sheets halfway through baking for even browning. Transfer sheets to wire racks and let stand until cookies firm up slightly, about 2 minutes. Then, transfer the cookies to wire racks and cool thoroughly.

Store, airtight, for 2 weeks, or freeze for up to 1 month.

NOTE: Be sure to buy hulled sesame seeds, available in health food stores. Unhulled ones have a dull, brownish appearance.

SNICKERDOODLES   *About 3 dozen 3½-inch cookies*

An old-fashioned New England favorite, these large, crinkly-topped sugar cookies are probably German in origin. Their nonsense name, which we've found children enjoy almost as much as the cookie itself, may be a corruption of the German word *Schneckennudeln*—which translates roughly as "crinkly noodles." Making its first appearance in *Joy,* this is yet another gem from our family friend Mildred Kroll of Lebkuchen fame.

Preheat the oven to 350°F. Grease cookie sheets.

Sift together:

2 cups (10 ounces) all-purpose flour
2 teaspoons cream of tartar
1 teaspoon baking soda
¼ teaspoon salt

Using an electric mixer, beat together until well blended and fluffy:

1 cup (8 ounces) unsalted butter, softened
1½ cups (10.5 ounces) sugar

Add and continue beating until well blended and smooth:

2 large eggs

Beat flour mixture into butter mixture until smoothly incorporated. Pull off pieces of the dough and roll between the palms to form generous 1¼-inch balls. Roll in a mixture of:

¼ cup (1.75 ounces) sugar
4 teaspoons cinnamon

Space about 2¾ inches apart on sheets. Bake, 1 pan at a time, in the upper third of the oven for 8 to 11 minutes, or until cookies are light golden brown around the edges. Rotate sheets halfway through baking for even browning. Transfer sheets to wire racks and let stand until cookies firm up slightly, 1 to 2 minutes. Then, transfer the cookies to wire racks and cool thoroughly. Cool cookie sheets between batches or cookies may spread too much.

Store, airtight, for 10 days, or freeze for up to 1 month.

MANDELBREZELN (ALMOND PRETZELS)

About 4 dozen pretzels

A sweet trompe l'oeil of a favorite snack, these small dessert pretzels are topped with a sprinkling of crunchy sugar in playful imitation of coarse salt. Chocolate fans should try the optional chocolate coating below.

Sift together:

> 1¾ cups (8.75 ounces) all-purpose flour
>
> ⅓ cup (1 ounce) powdered sugar
>
> ⅛ teaspoon salt

Stir in:

> ½ cup (2.5 ounces) blanched almonds, coarsely ground

Add and blend until a dough forms:

> 1 large egg, lightly beaten
>
> ¾ cup (6 ounces) unsalted butter, chilled and cut into bits
>
> grated zest of 1 lemon

Wrap the dough in plastic and chill at least 1½ hours.

To bake: Preheat the oven to 375°F. Grease cookie sheets, or line with parchment paper or greased aluminum.

Roll half the dough (keep remainder refrigerated) into a log 1 inch in diameter. Cut the log into 24 pieces. Roll each piece into an 8-inch-long rope, tapered at the ends, and shape into a pretzel. Repeat with remaining dough. Space pretzels 2 inches apart on sheets, and brush with:

> 1 large egg, lightly beaten

Sprinkle with:

> ½ cup (3.75 ounces) coarse sugar crystals or pearl sugar

Bake, 1 sheet at a time, for 12 to 15 minutes, until golden. (Alternatively, you may coat the pretzels with chocolate. If so, omit the egg wash and coarse sugar. Bake as directed and let cool. Melt chocolate as per Florentines Cockaigne, p. 43. Place each pretzel on a fork and dip into chocolate. Transfer to wax paper and let dry until chocolate is set.)

Store, airtight, for 1 week. If chocolate coated, store between layers of wax paper.

AMERICAN HOT COCOA

1 cup

Stir together in a heavy-bottomed saucepan:

> 1 tablespoon unsweetened cocoa
>
> 1 teaspoon sugar

Adding 1 tablespoon at a time, vigorously stir in:

> ¾ cup (6 liquid ounces) milk

When chocolate is a smooth paste, continue adding the milk slowly, stirring constantly to avoid scorching, over medium heat just until bubbles appear at the sides. Remove from the heat and add:

> ⅛ teaspoon vanilla, or ½ teaspoon Kahlúa or orange liqueur (optional)

Top each serving with:

> ground nutmeg, cinnamon, whipped cream, or marshmallows

ITALIAN HOT COCOA

2½ cups

In a medium heavy-bottomed saucepan briefly blend:

> ½ cup (2.5 ounces) unsweetened cocoa
>
> ⅓ cup (2.25 ounces) sugar
>
> 1 teaspoon cornstarch or arrowroot

Over a low flame stir in:

> ½ cup (4 liquid ounces) water

blending thoroughly. Add:

> ½ cup (4 liquid ounces) water
>
> 1 cup (8 liquid ounces) milk

Stir over low to moderate heat for 10 minutes, until the mixture thickens and coats a spoon. Stir in:

> ⅛ teaspoon vanilla, or ½ teaspoon Kahlúa or orange liqueur (optional)

Top each serving with:

> ground nutmeg, cinnamon, whipped cream, or marshmallows

Serve as is, or thin further with water, milk, or cream.

FRENCH HOT CHOCOLATE

6 generous cups

Chop into rough ¼-inch dice:

> 8 ounces bittersweet or semisweet chocolate

In a heavy-bottomed saucepan, bring to a rolling boil:

> 1 cup (8 liquid ounces) half and half

As soon as the surface is covered with bubbles, remove from the heat. Whisk in chocolate until the mixture is smooth. Strain the mixture through a fine sieve or clean tea strainer, pushing it through with a rubber spatula or wooden spoon. Store concentrate, airtight, for 10 days.

For each cup of hot chocolate, stir together:

> ¼ cup (2 liquid ounces) chocolate concentrate
>
> ¼ cup (2 liquid ounces) milk, water, or coffee

over low heat or in a microwave oven in a microwave-safe cup for 45 seconds to 1 minute. When liquid is warm but not boiling, add:

> ⅛ teaspoon vanilla, or ½ teaspoon Kahlúa or orange liqueur (optional)

Top each serving with:

> ground nutmeg, cinnamon, whipped cream, or marshmallows

Facing photograph: Chocolate- and sugar-coated Mandelbrezeln with American Hot Cocoa.

CANTUCCINI (TUSCAN ALMOND BISCOTTI)

About 3 dozen ½ x 3-inch biscotti

Big almond nuggets stud these crunchy cookies that Tuscans love to dip in their precious Vin Santo—a delicious and unusual wine made from semidry grapes, concentrated in flavor, often amber-colored, and usually sweet—but they're just as good dunked in milk, hot coffee, or tea. These particular biscotti (the name means "twice-cooked"), modeled after the northern Italian classic, are made from more of a thick batter than a dough. Handle it with a pastry scraper for greater ease.

Preheat the oven to 300°F. Butter and flour a cookie sheet.

Spread in a small baking pan and toast in the oven until evenly browned, stirring frequently:

> 2 cups (10.5 ounces) whole blanched almonds

Remove from the oven and set aside to cool completely. Using a sharp knife, chop ⅓ of the almonds into very large pieces and set aside. Transfer remaining almonds to a food processor fitted with a steel blade. Add and process until almonds are coarsely ground (like coarse sand):

> ¾ cup (3.75 ounces) all-purpose flour
> generous 1½ tablespoons shredded lemon zest
> 2 generous teaspoons shredded orange zest

Transfer to a bowl and stir in:

> ¾ cup (3.75 ounces) all-purpose flour
> 1 teaspoon baking powder

Combine in the food processor:

> ½ teaspoon salt
> pinch freshly ground pepper
> 2 large eggs
> 2 large egg whites
> 2 tablespoons light corn syrup
> ¾ cup (5.25 ounces) sugar
> 2 teaspoons vanilla

Process 5 seconds. Add dry ingredients and pulse a few seconds, just long enough to blend. Dough will be a dense batter—do not overmix. Using a rubber spatula and pastry scraper, spread the batter on the sheet and shape into 2 loaves, 3 inches wide x 16 inches long x 1 inch high. Space loaves about 3 inches apart.

Bake for 25 minutes. Remove from the oven and reduce heat to 325°F. Cool biscotti 10 minutes. When just cool enough to handle, place on a cutting board and cut crosswise, on a slight diagonal, into ½-inch-thick slices. Lay the slices flat on sheet.

Return to the oven and bake 12 minutes; turn slices over and bake another 15 minutes. Transfer biscotti to wire racks and let cool completely. Biscotti are best eaten the second day after baking and later.

Store, airtight, for 3 weeks, or freeze for up to 3 months.

Facing photograph: Cantuccini with Vin Santo.

CLASSIC BISCOTTI (REDUCED FAT)

About 3 dozen ½ x 3-inch biscotti

Most plain biscotti are low in fat to begin with. These have less than 2 grams each.

Preheat the oven to 375°F. Grease cookie sheet.

Using a wire whisk, thoroughly stir together:

 3⅓ cups (16.75 ounces) all-purpose flour

 2½ teaspoons baking powder

 ½ teaspoon salt

Using an electric mixer, beat together until very well blended:

 ¼ cup (2 liquid ounces) corn or canola oil

 1¼ cups (8.75 ounces) sugar

 2 large eggs plus 2 large egg whites

 1 teaspoon finely grated lemon zest

 ½ teaspoon finely grated orange zest

 1 teaspoon anise extract or almond extract

 1 teaspoon vanilla

Gradually mix the dry ingredients into the egg mixture until just thoroughly incorporated. Divide the dough in half. Shape each half into a smooth, evenly shaped 1½-inch-wide and 11-inch-long log, either by placing the log in sturdy plastic wrap and rolling it back and forth until smooth, or by shaping it with lightly floured hands. Arrange logs as far apart from one another as possible on sheet. Press logs to flatten slightly.

Bake on middle oven rack for 25 minutes. Transfer sheet to a wire rack. When just cool enough to handle, place on a cutting board and cut crosswise, on a slight diagonal, into ⅜-inch-thick slices. Lay the slices flat on sheet.

Return to the oven and toast 10 minutes. Turn the slices over and bake 5 to 10 minutes longer, or until lightly browned. Transfer the biscotti to wire racks and let stand until thoroughly cool.

Store, airtight, for 3 weeks, or freeze for up to 3 months.

CHOCOLATE MOCHA BISCOTTI

About 3½ dozen ½ x 3-inch biscotti

Preheat the oven to 350°F. Grease cookie sheet.

Spread in separate small baking pans:

 1⅓ cups (6.75 ounces) whole blanched almonds

 1⅓ cups (6.25 ounces) whole hazelnuts

Toast, stirring occasionally, until the almonds are tinged with brown and fragrant, and the hazelnut skins are loosened, 8 to 12 minutes. Let cool, then rub hazelnuts in a kitchen towel or between palms to remove as much skin as possible. Coarsely chop the nuts; set aside.

Chop into small bits:

 6 ounces bittersweet or semisweet chocolate

Set chocolate aside. Thoroughly stir together:

 3 cups (15 ounces) all-purpose flour

 ¼ cup (.75 ounces) unsweetened cocoa

 2½ teaspoons baking powder

 ¼ teaspoon salt

Using an electric mixer, beat together until very fluffy and well blended:

 ½ cup (4 ounces) unsalted butter, softened

 1 cup (7 ounces) sugar

Then, 1 at a time, add:

 3 large eggs plus 1 large egg white

 1½ tablespoons light corn syrup

 1 tablespoon instant coffee granules or powder

 1¼ teaspoons vanilla

 1¼ teaspoons almond extract (optional)

Continue beating until the coffee dissolves. Gradually mix the dry ingredients into the egg mixture until thoroughly incorporated. Stir in nuts and chocolate.

Divide the dough into 2 1½-inch-wide and 15-inch-long logs as for Classic Biscotti.

Bake on middle oven rack for 35 minutes. Transfer the sheet to a wire rack. When just cool enough to handle, carefully transfer logs to a cutting board and cut crosswise, on a slight diagonal, into ½-inch-thick slices. Lay the slices flat on the sheet.

Return to the oven and toast for 16 to 20 minutes, or until slices are almost firm when pressed on top. Transfer the biscotti to wire racks and let stand until thoroughly cool.

Store, airtight, for 3 weeks, or freeze for up to 3 months.

ABOUT ESPRESSO

By far the fullest body in any coffee is espresso, which is the name of a brewing method, not a coffee bean or shade of a coffee roast. The method is to force hot, but not boiling, water through finely ground coffee at high pressure. The pressure produces a syrupy body impossible to achieve by any other means, and a pleasantly bittersweet flavor that lingers on the palate for as long as twenty minutes.

The tradeoff for the matchless intensity of espresso is a very small amount of coffee to drink at a time. A properly brewed cup, or "shot," of espresso is just 1½ to 2 ounces, as compared with the 6 ounces of a standard cup of coffee as measured in the coffee industry—which most people consider to be half a cup of coffee. The brewing method does not change the caffeine content. One shot of espresso has about the same amount of caffeine as a 6-ounce cup of drip coffee.

Facing photograph: Classic Biscotti and Chocolate Mocha Biscotti with a cup of espresso.

ORANGE GINGER WAFERS (REDUCED FAT)

About 4½ dozen 2½-inch wafers

These crispy wafers have less than 1.5 grams of fat each.
Preheat the oven to 375°F. Lightly coat cookie sheets
with nonstick spray.
Using a wire whisk, mix thoroughly, then set aside:

  2 cups (10 ounces) all-purpose flour
  2 teaspoons baking powder
  ¼ teaspoon baking soda
  ½ teaspoon ground ginger
  ⅛ teaspoon ground cloves
  ¼ teaspoon salt

Using an electric mixer, beat together until well
blended and smooth:

  1 cup (7 ounces) sugar
  2½ teaspoons finely grated orange zest
  1 teaspoon finely grated lemon zest
  3 tablespoons corn or canola oil
  2½ tablespoons (1.5 ounces) unsalted butter,
  softened

Add and continue beating until well blended:

  1 large egg
  ¼ cup (2 liquid ounces) molasses
  2½ teaspoons vanilla

Gradually beat the dry ingredients into the egg mixture
until well blended and smooth. Pull off pieces of the
dough and roll between the palms, forming generous
¾-inch balls. Space 2¼ inches apart on cookie sheets.
Lightly oil the bottom of a large flat-bottomed drinking
glass. Very lightly dip the glass into:

  2 tablespoons sugar

Flatten balls until ¼ inch thick, dipping the glass into
the sugar before flattening each cookie. Wipe buildup
from glass and re-oil before continuing.
Bake, 1 sheet at a time, in the upper third of the oven for
8 to 11 minutes, or until wafers are just tinged with
brown and slightly darker around the edges. Rotate
sheets halfway through baking for even browning.
Transfer sheets to wire racks and let the cookies firm up
slightly, 1 to 2 minutes. Then, transfer cookies to wire
racks to completely cool. (Cool sheets between batches,
or dough will overheat and spread too much.)
Store, airtight, for 3 weeks, or freeze for up to 2 months.

GLAZED LEMON DAINTIES (REDUCED FAT)

About 3 dozen 1¾-inch cookies

These lemony morsels have 2 or so grams of fat each.
Preheat the oven to 350°F. Lightly grease cookie sheets.
Using a wire whisk, mix thoroughly, then set aside:

  2 cups (6.5 ounces) cake flour (not self-rising)
  1¼ teaspoons baking powder
  ⅛ teaspoon baking soda
  ½ teaspoon cream of tartar
  ¼ teaspoon salt

Using an electric mixer, beat together until very well
blended and smooth:

  3 tablespoons unsalted butter, softened
  3 tablespoons corn or canola oil
  1 tablespoon light corn syrup
  ⅓ cup (2.25 ounces) sugar

Add, beating until smoothly incorporated:

  1 large egg yolk
  2 tablespoons skim milk
  2 teaspoons vanilla
  ½ teaspoon very finely grated lemon zest

Gently stir the flour mixture into the egg mixture until
just smooth. Divide the dough into
quarters. With lightly greased
hands, roll each quarter into 9
equal balls, spacing about
1 inch apart on cookie
sheets.
Bake in the upper third
of the oven for 10 to 13
minutes, or until tops are
just barely firm to the
touch and faintly tinged
with brown. Transfer sheets to
wire racks until the cookies firm
up slightly, about 2 minutes.
Transfer cookies to wire racks until cool enough to
handle, about 10 minutes. Meanwhile, prepare the glaze
by stirring together until smooth and slightly fluid:

  1⅓ cups (4.25 ounces) powdered sugar, measured
  then sifted
  1 tablespoon plus 1 teaspoon fresh lemon juice
  ½ teaspoon light corn syrup
  ¼ teaspoon vanilla
  half a tiny drop of yellow food color (optional)

If necessary, thin the glaze with a few drops of water.
Dip the tops of the warm cookies into glaze, shaking off
excess. Return the cookies to the wire racks until glaze
sets, about 1 hour.
Store, airtight, between layers of wax paper, for 1 week,
or freeze for up to 1 month.

ABOUT FILLED COOKIES

Filled cookies—the fillings might be anything from jam tucked in the indentations of thumbprint cookies or homemade buttercream sandwiched between golden wafers to spiced dried fruit mixtures, chocolate thin mints or still-frozen ice cream—are often a bit time consuming to prepare, but they always give the impression of being "special."

Since there is so much variety in the shaping, handling and baking of filled cookies, not many general rules apply. Simply follow the directions provided with each recipe.

ALMOND THUMBPRINT COOKIES

(REDUCED FAT)   *About 3½ dozen 1¾-inch cookies*
With their pretty jam-filled centers and garnish of sliced almond bits, these dainty, light-textured thumbprint cookies, which contain only about 2 grams of fat apiece, are festive enough for a tea table. Be sure to use thick, seedless jam or preserves, not jelly, for the filling, or you'll have runny cookies.

Preheat the oven to 375°F. Lightly grease cookie sheets.
Using a wire whisk, thoroughly stir together, then set aside:

>1½ cups (7.5 ounces) all-purpose flour
>⅓ cup (1.5 ounces) cornstarch
>¾ teaspoon baking powder
>¼ teaspoon baking soda
>¼ teaspoon salt

Using an electric mixer, beat together until very well blended and smooth:

>3½ tablespoons (1.75 ounces) unsalted butter, softened
>3 tablespoons corn or canola oil
>1 tablespoon light corn syrup
>½ cup (3.5 ounces) sugar
>1 large egg
>¾ teaspoon very finely grated lemon zest
>2½ teaspoons vanilla
>¾ teaspoon almond extract

Beat the flour mixture into the egg mixture until just smooth. With lightly greased hands, pull off pieces of the dough and roll between the palms to form ¾-inch balls; don't make them larger, as the cookies should be small and will puff and spread a bit during baking. Place the balls on sheets about 2 inches apart. With the thumb (or knuckle), press down the center of each ball to make a large, deep well.

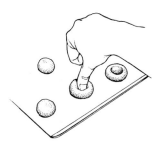

Fill the wells with:

>About ⅔ cup (7.25 ounces) seedless fruit jam or preserves, such as cherry, apricot, damson plum, or raspberry

Very lightly sprinkle the tops of the cookies with:

>2 to 3 tablespoons chopped sliced blanched or unblanched almonds

Bake on middle oven rack for 6 to 9 minutes, or until the tops are just barely tinged with brown. Transfer sheets to wire racks and let cookies firm up slightly, about 2 minutes. Then, transfer the cookies to wire racks until thoroughly cool.

Store, airtight, in 1 layer, for 10 days, or freeze for up to 1 month.

PECAN TASSIES   *Makes 24 2-inch tassies*

Reminiscent of pecan pie, only better! These tartlets are a snap to make. The recipe calls for using inexpensive mini muffin tins. If you happen to have individual tartlet tins, they would be even better here.

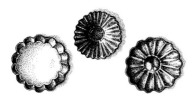

Combine in a food processor fitted with steel blade:

> 1 cup (4 ounces) pecan halves

With on/off pulses, chop pecans fairly fine; turn out into a medium bowl.

Combine in a food processor:

> 1⅓ cups (6.75 ounces) all-purpose flour
> ⅓ cup (1 ounce) powdered sugar
> ¼ teaspoon salt

Process in on/off bursts for about 5 seconds to mix. Sprinkle over the flour mixture:

> ½ cup plus 2 tablespoons (5 ounces) unsalted butter, chilled and cut into small pieces

Process in on/off pulses for about 20 seconds, or until the butter is cut into the dry ingredients and mixture resembles coarse meal. Processing in on/off pulses, add:

> 1 tablespoon plus 1 teaspoon ice water

Process in pulses until the dough just holds together; add a bit more water, if necessary, but do not over-moisten or overprocess. Remove the dough from processor.

(Alternatively, if processor is unavailable, chop the pecans by hand and set aside. Mix the flour and powdered sugar together. Sprinkle the butter over the top. Using a pastry blender, knives, or fingertips, cut the butter into the flour until the mixture resembles coarse meal. Sprinkle water over the top, tossing with a fork. Mix until the dough just holds together, adding a bit more water if necessary, but being careful not to over-moisten.)

Press the dough into a ball. Wrap in wax paper and refrigerate for 10 to 15 minutes.

To bake: Preheat the oven to 375°F. Generously coat 2 12-muffin mini muffin tins or 24 individual tartlet molds with nonstick spray.

Add to the reserved chopped pecans and beat with a fork until very well blended:

> ¼ cup (2 ounces) packed light brown sugar
> ⅓ cup (2.75 liquid ounces) dark corn syrup
> 1 large egg
> 1 tablespoon unsalted butter, melted
> 1 teaspoon vanilla

Remove the dough from refrigerator and divide in half. Divide each half into 12 equal portions. Roll the dough between the palms into smooth balls. Place the balls in the muffin tin cups or tartlet molds. Using a thumb or knuckle, form a very deep well in the center of each ball of dough. Press the dough upward from the bottom and sides so it extends to the rim of the cup all the way around, being careful not to break through the dough, as the filling will stick to the sides of the pan.

Spoon enough filling into each indentation to completely fill it without running over. Set the muffin tins or tartlet molds on a baking sheet. Bake in the upper third of the oven for 22 to 27 minutes, or until shortbread edges are browned and filling is puffed and set. (The filling sinks slightly as the tassies cool.) Transfer the muffin tins or tartlet molds to wire racks and let stand for about 15 minutes, or until the shortbreads have contracted from the sides of the pan and can be easily removed from the cups. Then, transfer the tassies to wire racks until thoroughly cool.

Store, airtight, in a single layer, for 1 week, or freeze for several months.

RUGELACH

About 30 cookies

This extraordinary cookie tastes as close to strudel as a cookie can. Always use jam or preserves, never jelly, with fruit and sugar (or high fructose) listed as the first two ingredients on the label, to avoid leaking during baking. Be sure to try chocolate chips for the raisins.

Cream on medium speed for 15 to 20 seconds, or just until well blended:

>   1 cup (8 ounces) unsalted butter, softened
>   6 ounces cream cheese, softened

Add all at once and mix on low speed for 10 to 15 seconds, or just until the dough comes together:

>   2¼ cups (11.25 ounces) all-purpose flour

Divide the dough into 3 equal pieces (½ pound each). Flatten each piece into a rectangle about 6 x 4 inches or into a 6-inch circle. Wrap in plastic and chill for 1 hour. (Dough may be refrigerated for up to 1 week or frozen in a plastic container for several months.)

Combine and set aside:

>   ⅓ cup (2.25 ounces) sugar
>   1 teaspoon ground cinnamon

To bake: Preheat the oven to 350°F. Line a cookie sheet with parchment paper. Work quickly with 1 piece of dough at a time, keeping the remaining pieces chilled. Generously sprinkle the rolling surface and the top of the dough with flour.

I. Shape rectangular rugelach by rolling each portion into a 10 x 16-inch rectangle, about ⅛ inch thick. Brush the excess flour from the top and bottom of the dough, and the rolling surface, and turn the rectangle so the long edge is parallel to the edge of the work surface. Leaving a ¼-inch border, spread each rectangle with:

>   ¼ cup (2.5 ounces) raspberry jam or apricot preserves (total needed: ¾ cup, 8 ounces)

Place a line of:

>   ¼ cup (1.25 ounces) raisins (total needed: ¾ cup, 4 ounces)

along the edge of the jam on the long side nearest you. Sprinkle the remaining jam with:

>   2 teaspoons of the cinnamon sugar (total needed: 2 tablespoons)
>   2½ tablespoons ground walnuts or ground blanched hazelnuts (total needed: ½ cup, 2 ounces)

Roll the dough, starting at the raisin edge, gently tucking and tightening as you go.

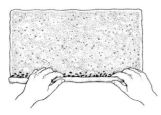

Finish with the seam of the roll facing down. Cut the cylinder into 1½ inch pieces.

Sprinkle each piece with:

>   ⅛ teaspoon of the cinnamon sugar

Bake for 25 minutes, or until bottom is light golden brown—the tops will still be blond. Cool completely.

II. Shape crescent rugelach by rolling each portion into a circle about 14 inches in diameter and about ⅛ inch thick.

Spread the jam in a thin layer, leaving a ¼-inch border, then sprinkle with the raisins, cinnamon sugar, and ground nuts. Cut the circle like a pizza pie, creating 8 (for large cookies) or 16 (for small cookies) even triangles.

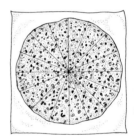

Roll up from the wide end to the point, tucking the point under.

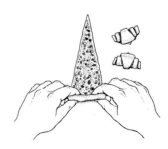

Sprinkle each piece with:

>   ⅛ teaspoon of the cinnamon sugar

Bake as for rectangular rugelach.

Store, airtight, for 1 week, or freeze for up to 3 months.

AUSTRIAN WREATHS
About 2 dozen cookies

These elegant morsels are two rings of butter cookies filled with apricot jam and topped with sliced almonds —a dazzler on the party table.

Grease cookie sheets, or line with parchment paper or greased aluminum foil.

Sift:

> ⅔ cup (2 ounces) powdered sugar

Add and cream together:

> 15 tablespoons (7 ounces) unsalted butter, softened

Add:

> 1 large egg yolk

Sift together and add gradually to above ingredients:

> 1¾ cups (8.75 ounces) all-purpose flour
> ¼ teaspoon ground cloves
> ¼ teaspoon cinnamon

Stir in:

> ¾ cup (3.75 ounces) blanched almonds, finely ground

Wrap the dough in plastic and chill for at least 1½ hours.

Divide the dough into quarters. Place each quarter between large sheets of wax paper and roll out ⅛ inch thick, checking the underside of the dough and smoothing any creases.

Working with 1 portion at a time, gently peel away and replace 1 sheet of the wax paper. (This will make it easier to lift the cookies from the paper later.) Peel away and discard the second sheet. (See illustrations, p. 49.) Use a 2½ inch cutter to cut rounds, then use a 1½ inch cutter to remove the centers from half the rounds, forming rings. Roll any scraps, cutting an equal number of rounds and rings. Arrange the shapes on separate cookie sheets and chill 1 hour.

To bake: Preheat the oven to 350°F.

Spread on a plate:

> 1 cup (3 ounces) sliced blanched or unblanched almonds

Brush 1 side of the rings with:

> 1 large egg white (2 tablespoons), beaten lightly

Press each glazed ring into the nuts, then turn almond-side up on the baking sheet. Bake rings for 10 to 12 minutes and rounds for 10 to 15 minutes, or until lightly browned. When cool, put through a strainer:

> ½ cup (5.5 ounces) apricot jam

Spread the rounds with the jam and top each with an almond-coated ring, pressing down lightly.

Store, airtight, between layers of wax paper, for 2 to 3 days, or freeze for up to 1 month.

DREI AUGEN
About 3 dozen 1½-inch cookies

The name means "three eyes" in German; the "eyes" are small holes in the top cookie, revealing the jelly within.

Cream together:

> 1¼ cups (10 ounces) unsalted butter, softened
> ⅔ cup (4.75 ounces) sugar

In a separate bowl, blend:

> 2⅓ cups (11.75 ounces) all-purpose flour
> ½ cup (2.5 ounces) unblanched almonds, finely ground
> 1 teaspoon cinnamon

Combine the dry ingredients with the butter. Divide the dough into thirds. Place each portion between large sheets of wax paper. Roll out each portion into a circle 11 inches in diameter and ⅛ inch thick, checking the underside of the dough and smoothing any creases. Keeping the wax paper in place, layer the rolled dough on a tray and refrigerate at least 2 hours and up to 24.

To bake: Preheat the oven to 350°F. Grease cookie sheets, or line with parchment paper or greased aluminum foil.

Working with 1 portion at a time (leave the other refrigerated), gently peel away and replace 1 sheet of the wax paper. (This will make it easier to lift the cookies from the paper later.) Peel away and discard the second sheet. (See illustrations, p. 49.) Using a 1½-inch round cutter, cut the cookies. Using the small end of a ⅜-inch plain pastry tip or a straw, cut out three small holes in half of the rounds. Transfer to cookie sheets, keeping the top and bottom cookies separate, as the cookies with holes bake faster. Bake on middle oven rack for 10 to 15 minutes, or until pale golden. Transfer sheets to wire racks. When cool, sift over the cut-out cookies:

> 1 cup (3.25 ounces) powdered sugar

Boil for 2 minutes:

> 1 cup (10.75 ounces) red currant jelly

Cool to lukewarm. Turn over the solid cookies so the bottom side is up. Spoon ¼ teaspoon of the cooled jelly onto each cookie, then top with a cut-out cookie and press gently so the jelly fills in the three holes.

Store, airtight, between layers of wax paper, for 2 to 3 days, or freeze for up to 1 month.

Facing photograph: Austrian Wreaths and Drei Augen.

CRANBERRY CHERRY PINWHEELS
(REDUCED FAT)
About 6 dozen 2¾-inch cookies

Made with lightly sweetened, dried cranberries and cherry preserves, these are colorful, eye-catching cookies with a pleasing crisp-chewy texture and zesty fruit taste. They are also extremely convenient, since the pinwheel logs may be held in the freezer for several weeks. Slicing and baking take only a few minutes.

Combine in a medium saucepan:

> 1½ cups (6 ounces) sweetened dried cranberries
> 1 cup (10.75 ounces) cherry preserves
> ¼ cup water
> ½ teaspoon ground cinnamon

Simmer, stirring frequently, for 5 to 8 minutes, or until the mixture is soft and most liquid is absorbed. If the mixture looks dry, stir in 1 tablespoon water. Transfer to a food processor and process until smooth. Cover and refrigerate until cool. (Filling may be stored up to 48 hours. Let return to room temperature and stir well before using.)

Using a wire whisk, thoroughly stir together and set aside:

> 3⅓ cups (16.75) all-purpose flour
> ¾ teaspoon baking powder
> ⅛ teaspoon baking soda
> ½ teaspoon salt
> ½ teaspoon ground cinnamon

Using an electric mixer, beat together until very well blended:

> ¼ cup (2 ounces) unsalted butter, softened
> 3 tablespoons corn or canola oil
> 1¼ cups (8.75 ounces) sugar
> 3 large egg whites
> 2 tablespoons milk
> 2 teaspoons vanilla
> 1½ teaspoons finely grated orange zest

Beat in half of the dry ingredients until just incorporated, then stir in the remainder until well blended. Divide the dough in half. Form each half into a rough oblong shape about 6 inches long. Center each log on a 12-inch-long sheet of wax paper. Cover with a second 12-inch-long sheet of wax paper. Press, then roll each log into an even 11-inch square, occasionally checking the underside of the dough and smoothing any creases. Patch the dough as necessary to make the sides relatively straight. Keeping the wax paper in place, layer the rolled dough on a tray and refrigerate until fairly firm, at least 30 minutes. (Dough may be held up to 24 hours; warm up slightly before using.)

To make pinwheels: Working with 1 square of dough at a time (leave the other refrigerated), peel away and discard the top sheet of wax paper. Spread half of the filling evenly over the entire surface of dough; the filling layer will be thin. Peeling off second sheet of paper as you work, tightly roll up the dough jelly-roll style. Gently stretch out the log center slightly to yield an even roll.

Wrap the roll in wax paper, twisting the ends to prevent unrolling. Place on a tray or cookie sheet. Repeat with the remaining dough. Freeze for 2½ hours or until the rolls are firm enough to be cut neatly. (If desired, freeze in plastic bags for up to a month; for easier slicing, allow the rolls to soften about 5 minutes before using.)

To bake: Preheat the oven to 375°F. Generously coat several cookie sheets with nonstick spray.

Using a large, sharp knife, cut the rolls crosswise into scant ¼-inch-thick slices. With a wide spatula, transfer the pinwheels to the cookie sheets, spacing about 1½ inches apart.

Bake in the upper third of the oven for 10 to 13 minutes, or until the edges are browned and the tops are lightly colored. Rotate sheets halfway through baking for even browning. Using a spatula, immediately transfer the cookies to wire racks. Let stand until thoroughly cool. Store, airtight, for 10 days, or freeze for up to 1 month.

CHOCOLATE MINT SURPRISES

About 2½ dozen 2¼-inch sandwich cookies

The filling for these luscious sandwiches comes in the form of thin chocolate mints, about 1½ inches across and no more than ⅛ inch thick. Thicker kinds, such as miniature mint patties, don't melt enough to bond with the cookies.

In contrast to most sandwich cookies, which are assembled after the wafers are completely cool, these must be put together while the cookies are still hot from the oven, so the chocolate will melt and stick to the cookie layers.

To dress up sandwich cookie tops, prick a decorative pattern with a dinner fork, enlarging the holes a bit by wiggling the tines back and forth.

Preheat the oven to 350°F. Lightly grease cookie sheets.

Combine in a large bowl:

> 2¼ cups (11.25 ounces) all-purpose flour
> 1 cup (8 ounces) unsalted butter, chilled but not firm and cut into small chunks

With a pastry blender, knives, or fingertips, cut the butter into the flour to form fine crumbs. Set aside.

Using a wooden spoon, beat until well blended:

> 2 large egg yolks
> ¾ cup (5.25 ounces) sugar
> ¼ teaspoon salt
> 1 teaspoon vanilla

Stir the egg yolk mixture into the flour mixture, then knead to form a smooth dough. Divide the dough in half and place each half between large sheets of wax paper. Roll out each half a generous ⅛ inch thick. Keeping the wax paper in place, layer the rolled dough on a tray. Chill in the freezer about 20 minutes, or until cold and slightly firm.

Working with 1 portion at a time, gently peel away and replace 1 sheet of the wax paper. (This will make it easier to lift the cookies from the paper later.) Peel away and discard the second sheet. (See illustrations, p. 53.) Cut out the wafers with a fluted or plain round 2¼-inch cutter (or the rim of a small drinking glass) or cut to a size just large enough that the commercial thin mint candies will fit within them. Using a spatula, carefully transfer the cookies from the wax paper to sheets, spacing about 1 inch apart. Roll any dough scraps between wax paper and continue cutting out cookies until all the dough is used; if the dough becomes too warm to handle, refrigerate it again briefly.

Bake in the upper third of the oven, 1 sheet at a time, for 9 to 14 minutes, or until just slightly colored on top and slightly darker at the edges. Rotate sheets halfway through baking for even browning. Transfer the sheets to wire racks and let the cookies stand until just firm enough to lift, but still hot. Then, working on the cookie sheet, turn half the cookies bottom up. Immediately cover each bottom with:

> 1 thin square chocolate mint wafer (about 30 total)

Cover each mint with the cookie tops, top up, and press down slightly. Let the sandwiches stand on the cookie sheets until the mints melt. Then, transfer the sandwiches to wire racks until the cookies are cool and the filling sets; during the cooling process, adjust any sandwiches that slip askew.

Store, airtight, in a single layer for 1 week, or freeze for up to 1 month.

PECAN MAPLE BUTTERCREAM SANDWICHES

About 3 dozen 2¼-inch sandwiches

The same rich dough for Chocolate Mint Surprises (p. 91) is matched here with the flavors of pecan and maple to give us these sublime cookies.

Preheat the oven to 350°F. Lightly grease cookie sheets. Spread in a baking pan and toast in the oven, stirring occasionally, 5 to 8 minutes, until very lightly browned:

   ½ cup (2 ounces) finely chopped pecans

Set aside to cool.

Prepare dough as for Chocolate Mint Surprises (p. 91), adding the toasted pecans to the dough with the egg mixture. Roll out and chill as directed. Cut cookies, using approximately 2¼-inch round or oval cutters. Using a spatula, transfer the cookies from the wax paper to the sheets, spacing about 1 inch apart. Roll any dough scraps between wax paper and continue cutting out cookies until all the dough is used. Garnish half of the cookies with:

   ¼ cup (1 ounce) finely chopped pecans

Pat down nuts to embed slightly. Bake in the upper third of the oven, 1 sheet at a time, for 9 to 14 minutes, or until lightly colored on top and slightly darker at the edges. Rotate sheets halfway through baking for even browning. Transfer the sheets to wire racks and let stand until cookies are slightly firm. Then, transfer cookies to wire racks to cool completely.

For maple buttercream filling, beat together until very light and fluffy:

   ⅓ cup (2.75 ounces) unsalted butter, slightly softened
   2¼ cups (7.25 ounces) powdered sugar, or more if needed
   2 tablespoons plus 2 teaspoons pure maple syrup
   ½ teaspoon vanilla

If buttercream is too thin, beat in more powdered sugar until a spreadable consistency is obtained. Spread about 1 measured teaspoonful of filling over cookie bottoms, then cover with cookie tops.

Store, airtight, in the refrigerator. Serve at room temperature within a day or two, as cookies gradually lose crispness upon standing.

GAZELLE'S HORNS

About 30 cookies

For the vegan in the family, here is a bite-size version of the best-loved pastry in Morocco.

Using a wire whisk, stir together thoroughly:

   2 cups (10 ounces) all-purpose flour
   ⅛ teaspoon salt

Stir in until a rough dough is formed:

   3 tablespoons olive or canola oil
   ¼ cup (2 liquid ounces) orange flower water or orange juice
   ½ cup (4 liquid ounces) water

Knead for five minutes, or until smooth and elastic. Wrap in plastic and chill for at least 1 hour.

Blend:

   1⅓ cups (6.75 ounces) almonds, finely ground
   ½ cup (3.5 ounces) sugar
   ½ teaspoon cinnamon
   1 tablespoon grated orange zest

Stir in:

   2 to 3 tablespoons orange flower water or orange juice

Knead gently until a smooth paste is formed.

To bake: Preheat the oven to 350°F. Line cookie sheets with parchment paper.

On a very lightly floured surface, roll the dough into a 16 x 18-inch rectangle. Cut into 6 strips, 3 inches wide x 16 inches long. Shape 1½ teaspoons of almond mixture into logs 1½ inches long. Evenly space 5 logs, end to end, along each strip of dough. Brush the dough lightly with water, then fold it over the almond logs, and press gently to seal. Use a pastry wheel to cut half moon shapes around the logs, beginning and ending at the folded edge. Gently bend each cookie into a crescent shape and prick the top with a fork.

Bake 20 to 25 minutes, until very lightly colored. Transfer sheets to wire racks and let cookies firm up slightly. Then, transfer cookies to wire racks to cool thoroughly. When cool, sift over the cookies:

   ½ cup (1.75 ounces) powdered sugar

Store, airtight, for 2 to 3 days, or freeze for up to 3 weeks.

ABOUT ICEBOX COOKIES

What Irma Rombauer first called "icebox cookies" in the 1931 *Joy*, and Marion Becker renamed "refrigerator cookies" in the 50s, might most accurately be called "freezer cookies" today, since the freezer is where we now store logs of slice-and-bake dough. But we've gone back to Irma's term, because it brings to mind a bygone era.

Icebox cookies are wonderfully convenient: The dough can be mixed when you have a few minutes, then formed into logs and stashed in the freezer (some for as long as 2 months) until you're ready to bake. There's little shaping time required, since the logs are simply cut crosswise into slices. Most kinds don't even have to be thawed before slicing—and actually slice best when very, very cold.

CREAM CHEESE ICEBOX COOKIES

About 3½ dozen 2¼-inch cookies

These cookies have a subtle but pleasing tang.
Thoroughly stir together and set aside:

   2 cups (10 ounces) all-purpose flour
   ½ teaspoon salt
   ½ teaspoon baking powder
   ⅛ teaspoon baking soda

Using an electric mixer, beat together until very fluffy and well blended:

   ⅔ cup (5.25 ounces) unsalted butter, softened
   1 cup (7 ounces) sugar
   1 large egg

Gradually beat in until thoroughly incorporated:

   3 ounces cream cheese, softened and cut
   into chunks
   1 teaspoon vanilla
   ¼ teaspoon finely grated lemon zest (optional)

Beat the flour mixture into the butter mixture until well blended. Refrigerate until slightly firm. Turn out onto a long sheet of wax paper. With well oiled hands, shape the dough into a 2-inch x 12-inch log. Roll up in the wax paper, twisting the ends to keep from unrolling. Place on a tray and freeze until firm, at least 3 hours.

To bake: Preheat the oven to 375°F. Grease cookie sheets.

Carefully peel off the wax paper. Cut the frozen log

Above: Cream Cheese Icebox Cookies decorated by using stencils or tiny cutters as design outlines for the nonpareils.

crosswise into ⅛-inch slices, then transfer the slices to cookie sheets, spacing about 2 inches apart. Using stencils or tiny cutters as a design outline, sprinkle the tops with:

   colored sugar, cinnamon sugar, or
   nonpareils

Press lightly to secure nonpareils in place. Bake for 7 to 11 minutes, or until edges are tinged with brown. Transfer sheets to wire racks and let cookies firm up slightly. Then, transfer the cookies to wire racks to cool completely.

Store, airtight, for 3 weeks, or freeze for up to 2 months.

ICEBOX SUGAR COOKIES

3½ to 4 dozen 2½-inch cookies

For busy moms or dads, these slice-and-bake logs are a cinch to make. Let the kids have a field day making them look Christmasy.

Thoroughly stir together, then set aside:

> 1½ cups (7.5 ounces) **all-purpose flour**
> 1½ teaspoons **baking powder**
> ¼ teaspoon **salt**

Using an electric mixer, beat until very fluffy and smooth:

> ⅔ cup (5.25 ounces) **unsalted butter, softened**
> ⅔ cup (4.75 ounces) **sugar**

Add and continue beating:

> 1 large **egg**
> 2 teaspoons **vanilla**
> ¼ teaspoon **finely grated lemon zest (optional)**

Beat in the flour mixture until just smoothly incorporated. Cover and refrigerate until slightly firm, 20 to 30 minutes. Place the dough on a long sheet of wax paper. With lightly oiled hands, shape into an even, 11-inch-long log. Roll up the wax paper, twisting the ends to keep from unrolling. Place on a tray and freeze until completely frozen, at least 3 hours. Use immediately or transfer to an airtight plastic bag and freeze for up to 1 month.

To bake: Preheat the oven to 375°F. Lightly grease cookie sheets.

Carefully peel the wax paper off the log. Cut into ⅛-inch-thick slices, then immediately transfer the slices to sheets, spacing about 2 inches apart.

Bake, 1 sheet at a time, on the upper oven rack for 7 to 10 minutes, or until cookies are golden all over and just slightly darker around the edges. The longer the baking time, the crisper the cookies. Transfer sheets to a wire racks and let cookies firm up slightly. Then, transfer the cookies to wire racks to cool completely.

Store, airtight, for 3 weeks, or freeze for up to 2 months.

Facing photograph: Icebox Sugar Cookies decorated with coated chocolate candies, nonpareil-coated candies, jellied candies, sprinkles, and nuts.

TWO MOONS

About 6 dozen cookies

Two elegant cookies from one recipe! The secret is a divided dough, one half of which takes pecans, the other chocolate.

Cream together:

> 15 tablespoons (7 ounces) unsalted butter, softened
> ⅔ cup (4.75 ounces) sugar

Add:

> 1 large egg, lightly beaten

Add, ¼ cup at a time:

> 2½ cups (12.5 ounces) all-purpose flour

Divide the dough in half. Wrap half in plastic and chill for 30 minutes. Divide the remaining dough in half. Knead into 1 piece:

> ⅓ cup (1.25 ounces) finely chopped pecans

Knead into the remaining piece:

> 1½ ounces finely chopped bittersweet or semisweet chocolate

Roll each flavored dough into a 10-inch-long cylinder. On a lightly floured surface, roll the chilled dough into an 11 x 9-inch rectangle, and cut in half lengthwise.

Brush with:

> 1 large egg, lightly beaten

Place 1 flavored cylinder in the center of each rectangle. Completely encircle each cylinder with the dough, gently smoothing the seams at the bottom and ends. Brush the logs with:

> 1 large egg, lightly beaten

and roll in:

> ½ cup (3.75 ounces) coarse sugar crystals

Wrap in plastic and chill for at least 4 hours.

To bake: Preheat the oven to 400°F. Line cookie sheets with parchment paper or greased aluminum foil. Slice each roll into 36 cookies and place on the sheets. Bake for 10 minutes, or until golden brown.

Store, airtight, for several days, or freeze for up to 1 month.

ABOUT PIPED, PRESSED & MOLDED COOKIES

The distinguishing feature of these cookies is that they're shaped with molds, presses, or other special equipment not generally on hand in the kitchen. Each type of shaping device lends a different, distinctive, and decidedly handsome look.

A pastry bag and piping tube can be used to shape a large variety of doughs; they simply need to be soft enough to flow through the decorator tip easily. Piped Spritz cookies, as well as a number of meringue cookies, can be quickly formed in this way.

For pressed cookies, such as Pressed Spritz, the dough can be short, but it must be chilled to just the right degree of firmness or the cookies won't squeeze out neatly in the desired shape. Too much baking powder or soda will cause the cookies to puff excessively.

With molded cookies such as Springerle and Spekulatius, the dough must be fairly firm to facilitate shaping, and thus contains little or no butter or leavening. Too much of either causes the cookies to spread and puff up during baking, blurring the splendid designs. And although there is no real way to produce the attractive look of these cookies without the appropriate molds, the dough can be rolled to about ⅜ inch thick and shaped with cookie cutters—for beautiful and equally delicious results! You can even try pressing a design into them with the head of an old-fashioned meat-tenderizing mallet, the surface of a deeply etched cut-glass bowl or tumbler, or even the tines of a fork.

Left and right: Spekulatius molds

Below: Three Springerle molds

PIPED & PRESSED SPRITZ COOKIES

About 5 dozen 2-inch cookies

No self-respecting Scandanavian baker is ever without a supply of Spritz dough in the refrigerator. Both piping and pressing work with this dough. For those who have never formed cookies with either method, piping is likely to yield better results with less practice. In fact, most cooks can turn out rosettes and stars that look as fancy as "store-bought" on the first try.

On the other hand, a press does yield cookies with a distinctive, charming appearance. Certainly if there is already a press in the house, it is fun and rewarding to put it to use. The key to success is to chill the dough just enough so the cookies can be forced through the press plate neatly and hold their shape during baking. Since most presses come with a variety of design plates—such as rosettes, stars, ridged strips, and Christmas trees—it is a good idea to try several and see which ones produce the most attractive results. (Keep in mind, with both piped and pressed cookies, any that don't come out quite right can be scooped up and formed again.)

Some spritz cookies are soft and tender to the point of being cakelike, but these are more on the crisp-tender side.

Using an electric mixer, beat until very fluffy and well blended:

> 1 cup (8 ounces) unsalted butter, softened
> ¾ cup (5.25 ounces) sugar

Add and beat in until evenly incorporated:

> 2 large egg yolks
> ¼ teaspoon salt
> 1½ teaspoons vanilla
> ¾ teaspoon almond extract (optional)

Sift over the butter mixture:

> 2¼ cups (11.25 ounces) all-purpose flour

Stir the flour into the batter until well blended. If planning to pipe the cookies, stir in:

> 1½ to 2½ tablespoons milk

until the dough is soft enough to easily force through a pastry bag and tube.

To pipe cookies: To ready the piping bag, fit with a ½-inch-diameter open star (or similar) tip. Then fill the pastry bag no more than two-thirds full, twist the opening tightly closed, and squeeze out cookies into generous 1½-inch rosettes or stars, spacing about 1 inch apart. (For best results, keep the bag and tip perpendicular to the baking sheet, with the tip almost touching the sheet.)

To press cookies: Do not thin the batter with milk, as it must be slightly firm. If it seems soft and difficult to handle, stir in 1 or 2 tablespoons of flour to firm it up. Cover and refrigerate the batter for 30 to 40 minutes, or until slightly stiff *but not at all hard.*

To ready the press, insert the desired design plate by sliding it into the head and locking it into place, or follow the manufacturer's directions. If you are unsure whether the dough is of the right consistency, put a small amount in the press tube and press out several test cookies. Chill the dough further before continuing if it does not go through cleanly. When the consistency is right, fill the press tube with dough, packing it down firmly. Press out cookies, spacing about 1 inch apart. Keep the unused dough refrigerated as you work.

If desired, decorate piped or pressed cookies with:

> candied cherry or almond bits, sprinkles, or
> nonpareils

At least 30 minutes before baking, preheat the oven to 350°F. Lightly grease cookie sheets.

Bake, 1 sheet at a time, in the upper third of the oven for 9 to 12 minutes, or until the cookies are just slightly golden and barely tinged with brown at the edges. Transfer sheets to wire racks and let cookies stand to firm up slightly. Then, transfer the cookies to wire racks to cool thoroughly.

Store, airtight, for 10 days, or freeze for up to 1 month.

Facing photograph: Piped Spritz Cookies decorated with candied cherries and sprinkles.

SPRINGERLE   *2 to 3 dozen assorted 2- to 4-inch cookies*

Springerle are striking-looking anise-flavored cookies made by stamping rolled-out dough with carved rolling pins or wooden molds. They are said to come from the old Swabian region of Germany. We love the way they look and often paint them with edible gold leaf (available at specialty baking stores) and hang them as decorations.

Have all ingredients at room temperature (68°F to 70°F).

Grease cookie sheets.

Thoroughly stir together:

   3¼ cups (16.25 ounces) all-purpose flour

   ¼ teaspoon baking powder

Whip with a mixer on high speed until lightened:

   4 large eggs

Beat 3 or 4 minutes longer, gradually adding:

   1⅔ cups (11.75 ounces) sugar

   1 teaspoon finely grated lemon zest

   1 teaspoon anise extract

Continue beating until the mixture is light, creamy, and thickened enough that it drops in thick ribbons when the beaters are lifted. Stir in the flour until smoothly incorporated.

Sprinkle a clean work surface with about:

   ¼ cup (1.25 ounces) flour

Turn out the dough onto the flour. Sprinkle additional flour over the dough. Knead in enough flour to firm up the dough and make it manageable. Divide the dough in half and place one half in a plastic bag to prevent it from drying out. Roll out the other portion ¼ inch thick, lifting the dough and lightly dusting the work surface and rolling pin as necessary.

Lightly dust a Springerle carved rolling pin (shown above) or cookie molds with flour; tap off the excess. Firmly roll or press the Springerle rolling pin or molds into the dough to imprint designs. Cut the designs apart using a pastry wheel or sharp knife. Using a spatula, transfer the cookies to sheets, spacing about ½ inch apart. Gather up the dough scraps and knead into the reserved dough. Then repeat the rolling and imprinting process until all the dough is used. Set the cookies aside, uncovered, for 10 to 12 hours.

To bake: Preheat the oven to 300°F.

If desired, sprinkle cookies with:

   2 to 3 tablespoons whole or crushed anise seeds

Depending on the size of the cookies, bake on middle oven rack for 18 to 25 minutes, or until almost firm but not colored. Transfer the cookies to wire racks and let cool at least 1 hour.

If desired, decorate cookies by highlighting the designs with a food color wash as follows: dilute food colorings with a bit of water and, using a small brush, apply a light wash of color to raised areas of the imprint. Let painted cookies stand until completely dry, about 2 hours.

Store, airtight, for 3 weeks—for a more pronounced anise flavor, add 1 or 2 teaspoons anise seed to the storage container—or freeze for several months.

Facing photograph: Unpainted Springerle. This page: Springerle painted with edible gold leaf.

SPEKULATIUS

1 to 2 dozen cookies, depending on size of molds

A Christmas specialty from the Rhineland, these cookies are also a favorite in Holland, where they are called *speculaas* and are sometimes made into figures as tall as 2 feet and given to children on December 6, the Feast of St. Nicholas.

Unlike Springerle molds, which imprint designs on the dough, Spekulatius molds serve as forms for it: A portion of dough is pushed into the carved-out indentation; the mold is then rapped on the counter to release the dough. If you don't have Spekulatius molds, use ceramic cookie molds stocked by kitchen boutiques at Christmastime.

Using a wire whisk, thoroughly stir together and set aside:

2¾ (13.75 ounces) cups all-purpose flour

1 tablespoon ground cinnamon

1¼ teaspoons ground allspice

¼ teaspoon ground nutmeg

Using an electric mixer, beat together until well blended and smooth:

¾ cup (6 ounces) butter, softened

1¼ cups (10 ounces) packed dark brown sugar

1 large egg

1 tablespoon milk

2 teaspoons vanilla

¼ teaspoon almond extract

½ teaspoon finely grated lemon zest

Mix in the dry ingredients until evenly incorporated. Wrap the dough in plastic and refrigerate at least 8 hours and up to 3 days. (The dough may also be frozen for up to a month. Thaw it completely in the refrigerator before using.)

To bake: Preheat the oven to 350°F. Grease cookie sheets. Using a pastry or basting brush, prepare the molds by lightly brushing vegetable oil over all interior surfaces, being sure to reach all the crevices and indentations. Lightly sprinkle or sift flour over the molds, tipping molds back and forth until all the crevices are coated. Tap out all excess flour. Molds must be dusted after each cookie, but do not need to be re-oiled.

Working with a small portion of the dough at a time (leave the remainder refrigerated), pull off pieces large enough to fill the mold, and press the dough into the form. Even if the dough seems too stiff at first, work with it; it will soften as the cookie is formed. When the interior is completely filled, press down all over to remove air pockets. Push any dough protruding over the edges back inside the edges of the mold. Using a large, sharp knife, cut away the excess dough so the cookie is flush with the back of the mold.

To remove cookie from a *wooden* mold, hold it upside down and rap it repeatedly and sharply against a hard surface until the cookie loosens.

For a *ceramic* mold, rap it a little more gently against a wooden board or other slightly softer surface to avoid chipping or breaking the form.

When the cookie is loosened all over, tap or peel it out onto the sheet. If one particular section sticks, very carefully loosen it with the point of a paring knife. Space cookies about 1½ inches apart.

Bake on middle oven rack for 15 to 25 minutes, depending on the size of the cookies, until they are tinged with brown around the edges. Transfer sheets to a wire racks and let stand several minutes until cookies firm up. Then, transfer cookies to wire racks to cool completely. Store, airtight, for 3 weeks, or freeze for several months.

Spekulatius molds

KEEPSAKE COOKIES

About 1½ dozen 2¼-inch ornaments

In our house, the most beloved ornaments in the stash of Christmas ornaments that were brought out every year were the ones we had made from this indestructible cookie-like salt dough. Once the dough has been cut out, baked and dried, the ornaments can be decorated with acrylic paints or glued-on sparkles.

Combine in a food processor fitted with a metal blade:

> **2 cups (10 ounces) all-purpose flour**
> **1 cup (10 ounces) table salt**

Process for 2 to 3 minutes, until well blended and salt is powder fine.

Add, pulsing until evenly incorporated:

> **⅔ cup (5.25 liquid ounces) water**

Process 30 seconds longer, until dough is smooth and malleable. If dough is dry, add a bit more water; if too wet, add a bit more flour. Pulse just until mixture is well blended and smooth. Place in an airtight plastic bag. Let stand at room temperature at least 12 hours and up to 4 days before handling.

To bake: Preheat the oven to 200°F. Line a cookie sheet with aluminum foil, shiny side visible.

Roll out dough a scant ¼ inch thick on lightly floured surface. Dip edges of cookie cutters into vegetable oil to prevent them from sticking to dough. Cut out cookies. For more elaborate ornaments, use mini cutters to form cutouts in cookies.

Transfer to sheets, spacing several inches apart. Form holes for threading ribbon and hanging the finished ornaments by poking a hole with a toothpick through the ornaments; leave toothpick in place during baking. Bake 30 to 45 minutes, or until cookies are very firm. Turn over and bake on second side until firm, 30 to 45 minutes. Transfer sheets to wire racks and let stand 24 hours to complete drying.

Decorate the cookies with:

> **acrylic paints in assorted colors or glue-on sparkles**

Packed carefully in a cardboard box and kept in a cool, dry place, Keepsake Cookies will last for years.

NOTE: Trace the shapes below to make templates. See p. 49 for directions.

Facing photograph, left to right: Keepsake cookies in the shape of a snowman, mitten, and Christmas stocking.

GINGERBREAD HOUSE

8-inch-wide x 9-inch-tall house

A decorated homemade gingerbread house is a magical presence on a holiday table or in front of the fireplace. For best results, keep all the dough pieces as straight and true to their patterns as possible. Just as in real home construction, uneven and crooked "boards" will yield a wobbly, jerry-built structure. Of course, the icing and candy add-ons can be as gaudy and overdone (or as refined and understated!) as the decorators wish. Although gingerbread houses are most often associated with Christmas, you can create a gingerbread Easter bunny hutch or Halloween witch's cottage just by changing the decorations in this recipe.

GINGERBREAD DOUGH

Using a wire whisk, thoroughly stir together, and set aside:

6 cups (30 ounces) all-purpose flour
½ teaspoon baking powder
1 tablespoon plus 1 teaspoon ground ginger
1 tablespoon plus 1 teaspoon ground cinnamon
½ teaspoon ground cloves or ground allspice
½ teaspoon salt

Using an electric mixer, beat together until smooth and fluffy:

¾ cup (6 ounces) unsalted butter, softened
1½ cups (12 ounces) packed light brown sugar

Beat in until well blended:

2 large eggs
1 cup (8 liquid ounces) dark molasses
1 tablespoon water

Beat half of the flour mixture into the molasses mixture until incorporated. Stir in remaining flour then knead mixture until well blended. If the dough is soft, stir in more flour until it is firmer and more manageable but not at all dry.

Place dough in an airtight plastic bag or plastic container. Set aside in a cool place, but not the refrigerator, for at least 2 hours and up to 6. Or refrigerate for several days, allowing the dough to return to room temperature before using.

CUTTING OUT PATTERN PIECES

Meanwhile, cut out pattern pieces using either graph paper or smooth, manila folder–weight paper. Graph paper lines provide easy, automatic guides for measuring and cutting out pattern pieces, but slightly heavier paper yields sturdier patterns. Cut out and label pattern pieces as follows (see illustrations, p. 109):

1 5½-inch-wide x 7½-inch-high piece for front and back
1 7-inch-wide x 6½-inch-high piece for roof
1 5-inch-wide x 3-inch-high piece for house sides

To form peaked front and back: With a pencil, mark the center point on one of the short ends of the 7½ x 5½-inch rectangle to establish the top of the template. Starting at the left-hand bottom corner, measure 3 inches up the side and mark this point. Repeat on the right-hand side. Using a ruler, connect the left-hand mark with the center top mark. Repeat on the right-hand side, creating an inverted V (see illustration, p. 109). Cut along these lines to create the front and back peaked template.

For chimney, cut out pieces as follows:

1 1-inch-wide x 3-inch-high piece for chimney front
1 1-inch-wide x 1½-inch-high piece for chimney back
1 1-inch-wide piece, 2¾ inches high on one side and 1½ inches high on the other (as shown in illustration, p. 109)

ROLLING OUT DOUGH

Preheat the oven to 350°F. Have ready several large cookie sheets.

Divide the dough in half. Working with only half at a time (leave the other half covered to prevent drying), roll out dough a scant ¼ inch thick directly on large sheets of parchment paper; keep the layer as uniform as possible. This is easier if you have a set of ¼-inch dowels to lay on all four sides of the dough and use as guides, but these are not essential. If necessary, lightly dust rolling pin with flour to prevent sticking.

CUTTING OUT HOUSE PIECES

Before placing pattern pieces on dough, lightly rub surface with a small amount of flour. Gently lay as many pattern pieces as will fit on the dough.

Using a sharp knife, wiping the blade as you work, cut out the following pieces: house front, back, and 2 sides. Cut away front door opening as shown in illustration, p. 109, reserving the door piece. If desired, also cut away centered upstairs window; then split cutout piece in half lengthwise to use as shutters. Also cut out chimney front, back, and side pieces. For sides, cut around angled pattern piece, then turn pattern over and cut out again.

Facing photograph: Gingerbread House surrounded by sugar "snow" and decorated with coated chocolate candies, sweet-and-sour dots, coated licorice, chewing gum squares, and a ready-made candy wreath, available at specialty candy stores.

Immediately lift patterns from the surface to prevent sticking, and set aside. Peel away excess dough from around cutout pieces, reserving all scraps in a plastic bag to prevent drying. As necessary, cut apart parchment with scissors so individual house pieces (along with parchment) can be transferred to baking sheets; group large house pieces together on larger cookie sheets, and chimney pieces, door and shutter pieces, if using, together on a smaller sheet, spacing pieces about 1 inch apart.

(Alternatively, if parchment is unavailable, on a lightly floured work surface, roll out dough a scant ¼ inch thick, being careful to keep layer uniform. Lift dough frequently and lightly dust pin with flour as needed to prevent sticking. Before placing pattern pieces on dough, lightly rub surface with a small amount of flour. Gently lay as many pattern pieces as will fit on the dough. Using a wide spatula, gently transfer pieces from work surface to cookie sheet, trying not to stretch them out of shape. If pieces do stretch, trim them back to original pattern size using a paring knife; remove scraps from baking sheet. Reserve all scraps in a plastic bag. Continue rolling out dough portions and cutting out until all pieces are prepared.)

If desired, add curved roof tile design to roof pieces by pressing the curve of a flatware spoon into the dough surface to produce indentations at regular intervals (see illustration, p. 109). If desired, add clapboard texture to house sides, front and back by drawing the back of a dinner fork horizontally across dough surface so the tines produce lines.

BAKING THE HOUSE PIECES

Bake larger house pieces 11 to 15 minutes and chimney and door pieces 6 to 8 minutes, until just tinged with brown and beginning to darken at the edges. Remove sheets to wire racks and let stand for 15 minutes, or until pieces are cool and firm. Gently transfer the pieces along with parchment to wire racks and let stand until completely cooled.

Store, airtight, for several weeks, or freeze up to several months for longer storage. Store large pieces completely flat to prevent breakage.

MAKING THE ICING

Royal Icing is the glue for constructing your gingerbread house. The recipe yields enough for both gluing and for decorating the finished house with "snow" or other finishing piping. The icing can be made up to 4 days ahead and refrigerated, tightly covered, until needed.

I. ROYAL ICING

To avoid using uncooked egg whites, make the royal icing for the gingerbread house with meringue powder. Of course, if the icing will be used only as decoration and not eaten, it may be more convenient to prepare it with egg whites. In this case, simply substitute a generous ¼ cup of egg whites, completely free of egg yolk for the meringue powder/water mixture called for below. If you cannot find meringue powder but still wish to avoid using raw eggs, make the cooked Royal Icing below. Color icing, if desired, with drops of food coloring; or for much bolder and brighter results, color with powdered coloring or food paste color (color intensifies as it stands).

In a large mixing bowl beat on low speed until frothy:

> 2 tablespoons meringue powder mixed with ¼ cup warm water
> ¼ teaspoon freshly squeezed lemon juice

Gradually beat in:

> 2½ cups (8.25 ounces) powdered sugar plus more as needed

Whip on high speed until mixture stands in stiff peaks and is very glossy, 3 to 5 minutes. If mixture is too stiff to spread easily, beat in a bit of water; if too runny, beat in a bit more powdered sugar. Cover the bowl of icing with a damp tea towel to prevent it from drying out during house assembly and decoration. Store, tightly covered and refrigerated, for up to 4 days.

II. COOKED ROYAL ICING

In a microwave-proof bowl, stir until thoroughly combined:

> 2 large egg whites
> 1⅓ cups (4.25 ounces) powdered sugar

Microwave on high until the mixture reaches 160°F but does not exceed 175°F on an instant-read thermometer, about 1½ to 2 minutes. Check every 30 to 45 seconds, remembering to remove the thermometer before restarting the microwave. If the first temperature readings do not reach 160°F, wash the thermometer thoroughly before taking additional readings. Add:

> 1⅓ cups (4.25 ounces) powdered sugar

Using an electric mixer, beat at high speed until the icing is cool and holds stiff peaks when beaters are lifted.

CONSTRUCTING THE HOUSE

If you have a pastry bag and large writing tube, apply the icing glue with it. Otherwise, apply it as neatly as possible using a spoon or the tip of knife.

Working on a large wax paper–lined tray, start by putting house front, sides, and back together. Pipe a line

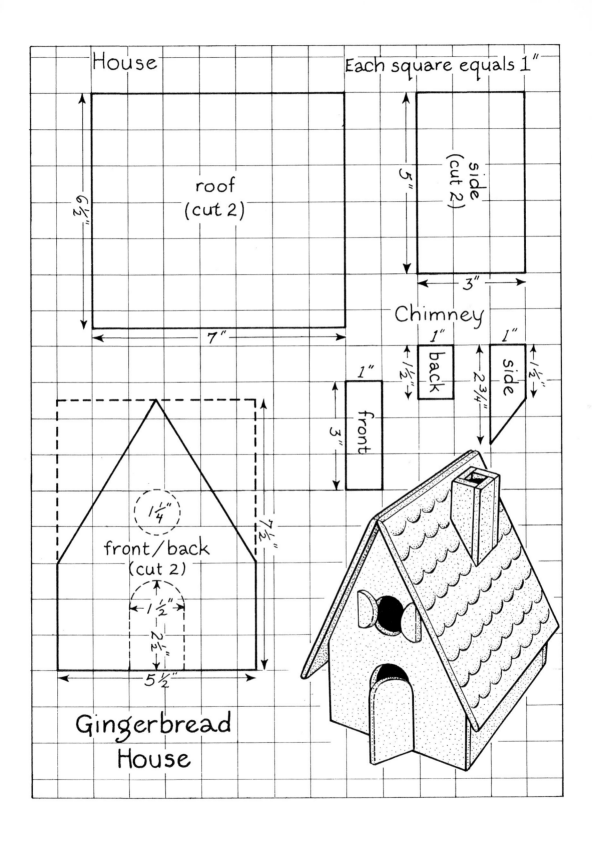

House

Each square equals 1"

roof
(cut 2)

6½"

7"

side
(cut 2)

5"

3"

Chimney

1" back

½"

1" side

2¾"

½"

1" front

3"

front/back
(cut 2)

1¼"

7½"

1½"

2½"

5½"

Gingerbread
House

of icing on each end of 1 side piece. Place it between the front and back pieces, gently pressing at joints to lightly hold in place until second side is added. Add icing to the second side piece and fit in place between front and back, adjusting as necessary to make the house square.

Working on one side of the house at a time, pipe icing along angled front and back edges. Grasp 1 roof piece by the edges and lay it against the piped edges, gently pressing to lightly hold it in place until second roof piece is added. To finish the roof, pipe icing along angled front and back edges as well as the top edge of the roof piece already in place. Press second piece in place, adjusting so it fits snugly against the first roof piece to form a peak.

Force additional icing into any seams that need reinforcing, wiping off excess with a fingertip.

For chimney, glue the 4 pieces together as for the house base. Before icing the base, set chimney in place on the rooftop. If it does not sit up straight, carefully trim chimney bottom with a sharp knife until the bottom angle aligns evenly with the rooftop. Then pipe icing on the base of the chimney and secure it in place on rooftop.

DECORATING THE HOUSE

Let the house stand, uncovered, at least 1 hour, and preferably overnight, before decorating.

Decorate according to the season. For Christmas you may want to add royal icing snow and icicles along the edges of the roof and accent the house with candy canes, peppermint pinwheels, and other appropriate sweets. For an Easter bunny hutch, snow should be omitted and replaced by pastel-tinted icing to cover seams and to accent roof lines. Candies could include miniature eggs, jelly beans, Jordan almonds, and tiny chocolate bunnies. A Halloween cottage might feature harvest colors, shredded wheat thatched roof and seasonal goodies like tiny pumpkin-shaped candies, licorice sticks, shelled nuts, and candy corn.

Whatever the theme, when used generously, icing can go far in camouflaging smudges and crooked seams. It looks best when piped using a pastry bag and small open star tip, but children will be perfectly happy spooning it in place and covering any messy spots by piling on candies and nonpareils.

Decorating will be most enjoyable and creative if you have on hand an abundant assortment of suitable candies, colored sugar, and sprinkles. For several different colors of icing, divide the batch into bowls and tint each with food color. (Cover bowls with plastic wrap when not being used, and add a drop of water if the icing becomes too thick at any point.) Then decorate your gingerbread house to your heart's content.

ABOUT EXTRAS

Cookies aren't the only treat folks enjoy making and eating during the holidays, of course. Candied orange slices, pralines, candied popcorn, and other such delights help make the season bright—and we could scarcely imagine Christmas without fruitcake, stollen, and, of course, steamed Christmas Pudding with hard sauce.

CANDIED POPCORN

About 6 cups

Have ready in a large bowl:

> 6 cups (1 ounce) popped corn

Prepare either of the syrups below. Remove the syrup from the heat and pour it over the corn, covering it well. Stir gently with a wooden spoon until the corn is completely coated, then turn the corn out onto a cookie sheet lined with wax paper. When cool enough to handle with lightly buttered fingers, separate into individual kernels or press into balls or into a well-oiled mold. Store, airtight, at room temperature for 10 days.

WHITE SUGAR SYRUP

Combine in a small heavy saucepan:

> ⅔ cup (5 ounces) sugar
>
> ½ cup water
>
> 3 tablespoons light corn syrup
>
> ⅛ teaspoon salt
>
> ¼ teaspoon distilled white vinegar

and cook over low heat, stirring constantly, until sugar is completely dissolved. Brush down the sides of the pan with a damp pastry brush or wipe with a damp paper towel to prevent sugar from crystallizing. Place a candy thermometer in the pan, raise the heat to medium, and cook, without stirring, until it reaches the high end of the soft-crack stage, 290°F.

MOLASSES SYRUP

Melt in a small heavy saucepan:

> 1 tablespoon unsalted butter

Add:

> ½ cup (4 liquid ounces) light molasses
>
> ¼ cup (1.75 ounces) sugar

and cook over low heat, stirring constantly, until sugar is completely dissolved. Brush down the sides of the pan with a damp pastry brush or wipe with a damp paper towel to prevent sugar from crystallizing. Place a candy thermometer in the pan, raise the heat to medium, and cook, without stirring, until it reaches the high end of the soft-crack stage, 290°F.

CALIFORNIA FRUIT CAKE

One 9 x 5-inch or two 8 x 4-inch loaves

Nuts and dried fruits only need apply; candied and glacéed fruits are banished. We never soak this cake with liquor, yet it keeps for weeks if it's wrapped well. Slice very thin!

Preheat the oven to 300°F. Line the bottom and sides of one 9 x 5-inch or two 8 x 4-inch loaf pans with parchment paper.

Mix together in a large bowl:

> ¾ cup (3.75 ounces) all-purpose flour
>
> ¼ teaspoon baking soda
>
> ¼ teaspoon baking powder
>
> ½ teaspoon salt

Add and mix thoroughly with your fingers:

> ¾ cup (6 ounces) packed light or dark brown sugar
>
> 1 packed cup (5.5 ounces) dried apricot halves
>
> 2 cups (12 ounces) quartered dates
>
> 3 cups (10 ounces) walnut halves

In a small bowl, beat until light:

> 2 large eggs
>
> 1 teaspoon vanilla

Pour the egg mixture over the dry ingredients and mix, using your hands, until all of the fruit and nut pieces are coated. Scrape into the pan and bake about 1 hour and 10 to 20 minutes for the smaller loaves or 1 hour and 30 to 40 minutes for the larger loaf, or until the top is deep golden brown and the batter clinging to the fruit and nut pieces seems set. Tent loosely with foil if the loaves brown too early. Cool in the pan on a wire rack for 5 to 10 minutes before unmolding to cool thoroughly on the rack.

Wrap, airtight, and store at least 3 days before serving!

LINZERTORTE
10 to 12 servings

This classic Austrian pastry improves with age. Be sure to hide it well if you want it to stay around long enough for its flavors to develop! Serve *mit schlag* (with whipped cream). If you want the cream to sit out on your buffet table without separating, make the stabilized whipped cream.

Preheat the oven to 350°F.

Sift together:

> 1⅓ cups (6.75 ounces) all-purpose flour
> ½ cup (1.75 ounces) powdered sugar
> ½ teaspoon ground cinnamon
> ¼ teaspoon ground cloves
> ¼ teaspoon salt

Spread in a baking pan and toast in the oven, stirring occasionally, 5 to 8 minutes, until very lightly browned:

> ¾ cup (3 ounces) sliced almonds or hazelnuts

If using hazelnuts, rub in a towel to remove skins. Set aside to cool completely. Turn off oven. Finely grind and add to the flour mixture. Stir in:

> 2 large egg yolks

Add:

> 10 tablespoons (5 ounces) unsalted butter, softened
> 2 teaspoons chopped lemon zest

Mix until completely combined. Wrap the dough in plastic wrap and refrigerate for several hours to overnight.

To bake: Preheat the oven to 350°F. Have ready a 9-inch tart pan with removable bottom.

Remove the dough from the refrigerator and let sit at room temperature until no longer hard, about an hour. Set aside a quarter of the dough for the lattice. With your hands, evenly press the dough into the bottom and sides of the tart pan. Roll the remaining dough between 2 sheets of plastic wrap. Remove the top sheet and cut the dough into pencil-thin strips. Refrigerate both until firm. Fill the tart with:

> 1½ cups (16.25 ounces) raspberry jam

Carefully place half of the strips across the tart at equal distance from each other, pinching the edges to the crust. Arrange the remaining strips on top, placing them at right angles to the first layer. Each strip does not have to be in a single piece, it can be pieced together. Bake for 40 to 45 minutes, until golden brown.

Transfer to a wire rack and let cool completely. Remove sides, leaving bottom of pan in place under the torte. Store, airtight, in the refrigerator, for up to 1 week, or freeze for 1 month. Bring to room temperature before serving.

NOTE: For a spicier, chocolate crust, increase the cinnamon to 1½ teaspoons, increase the ground cloves to a generous ⅓ teaspoon, and add 1 tablespoon of unsweetened cocoa to the dry ingredients in the above recipe.

WHIPPED CREAM
2½ to 3 cups

Beat until thickened:

> 1 cup (8 liquid ounces) chilled heavy cream
> ½ teaspoon vanilla

Add and beat until stiff enough to spread:

> 2 teaspoons to 2 tablespoons sugar to taste, or 1 to 4 tablespoons sifted powdered sugar, or 2 teaspoons honey

STABILIZED WHIPPED CREAM

For the freshest flavor, in the best of all worlds, desserts filled or frosted with whipped cream are enjoyed on the same day that they are prepared. In reality we sometimes need to work in advance. The best quality heavy cream is 38 to 40 percent butterfat and may be used to fill or frost a cake, even a day in advance, without adding a stabilizer. But this type of cream is not available everywhere. Gelatin added to whipped cream gives it a firmer mousse-like texture and keeps it from weeping. It must still be stored in the refrigerator, but it will hold up longer on a buffet table and you may frost or fill a cake with it a day in advance without worry.

In a heat proof cup, sprinkle:

> ½ teaspoon gelatin

over:

> 1 tablespoon cold water

Let soften for 5 minutes without stirring. Place the cup in a pan of simmering water until the gelatin is melted and the liquid looks clear. Cool to room temperature. Beat cream with vanilla as described, adding the cooled, but not cold, gelatin mixture as the cream begins to thicken.

STOLLEN (CHRISTMAS LOAF)   *2 loaves*

This traditional Christmas bread is made in various shapes and sizes and is turned out at Christmastime even in kitchens not known for their baking. Perfect for Christmas morning feasting and as a gift.

Preheat the oven to 350°F. Grease 2 cookie sheets.

Have ready:

> 6 to 8 cups (30 to 40 ounces) all-purpose flour

Combine and let stand for 3 to 5 minutes:

> 1½ cups (12 liquid ounces) lukewarm water or milk
>
> 2 packages active dry yeast

Add 1 cup of the flour. Cover this sponge and let it rest in a warm place until light and foamy, about 1 hour. Sprinkle a little of the sifted flour over:

> ½ pound (8 ounces) raisins
>
> ½ pound (8 ounces) chopped blanched almonds
>
> ½ cup (2.5 ounces) chopped candied fruits (optional)

Beat until soft:

> 1½ cups (12 ounces) unsalted butter

Add gradually and blend until light and creamy:

> ¾ cup (5.25 ounces) sifted sugar

Beat in, one at a time:

> 3 large eggs

Add:

> ¾ teaspoon salt
>
> ¾ teaspoon grated lemon zest

Add the sponge and enough flour to knead the dough until smooth and elastic. Cover and let rise until doubled in bulk. Toss it onto a floured board. Knead in the fruit and nuts. Divide the dough into 2 equal pieces. Roll each into an 8 x 15-inch oval. Fold in half lengthwise and place loaves on greased baking sheets. Brush the tops with:

> Melted butter

Let the loaves rise, covered, until they again almost double in bulk, about 45 minutes.

Preheat the oven to 350°F. Bake 30 to 40 minutes, or until loaves sound hollow when tapped on the bottom. When cool, sprinkle with powdered sugar or brush with Milk or Lemon Glaze, below.

Store, airtight, at room temperature, for 1 week, or freeze for up to 3 months.

MILK GLAZE

Sift:

> ½ cup (1.5 ounces) powdered sugar

Add:

> 2 teaspoons hot milk
>
> ¼ teaspoon vanilla

LEMON GLAZE

Mix or blend:

> 1¼ cups (4 ounces) powdered sugar
>
> ¼ cup (2 liquid ounces) freshly squeezed lemon, orange, or lime juice
>
> 1 teaspoon vanilla

MULLED WINE   *4 servings*

This warming brew is particularly appreciated on wintry nights.

Place in a saucepan, covered, over low heat:

> 1 bottle (750 ml) California Merlot or other dry red wine
>
> 4 sticks cinnamon
>
> peel of 1 orange, cut into 4 pieces
>
> 3 to 4 tablespoons granulated sugar

Simmer for 20 to 30 minutes, then ladle into warmed mugs, placing a cinnamon stick and piece of orange peel in each.

To make *vin brûlé,* a French variation on mulled wine, bring the same ingredients to a boil over high heat, then uncover and carefully ignite with a long match. When the flame has died down, remove mixture from heat and ladle into warmed mugs, garnishing them as above. The French say this drink is better than aspirin to ward off the grip of a cold as well as the night chill.

MULLED CIDER   *4 servings*

A tasty alternative to Mulled Wine. A nonalcoholic version may be made by omitting the rum.

Place in a saucepan over low heat:

> 2 jiggers (3 liquid ounces) light or dark rum
>
> 1 bottle (750 ml) clear, nonalcoholic apple cider
>
> 4 sticks cinnamon
>
> peel of 1 orange, cut into 4 pieces
>
> 1 tablespoon granulated sugar

Simmer for 20 to 30 minutes, then ladle into warmed mugs, placing a cinnamon stick and piece of orange peel in each.

Facing photograph: Stollen, sprinkled with powdered sugar, and Mulled Wine.

STEAMED PLUM PUDDING (CHRISTMAS PUDDING)

One 7 to 8 cup mold or two 3½ to 4 cup molds

Of all Christmas desserts, none is more Victorian than a fine homemade plum pudding, especially when brought to the table in a blue blaze of brandy flames. Plum is an old English term for raisins, hence the name. Serve hot with hard sauce, below.

Divide in half and chop one half coarsely:

2⅔ cups (16 ounces) dark raisins

Combine all the raisins in a heavy-bottomed pot with:

2 cups (10 ounces) currants (small raisins)

2 cups (16 liquid ounces) water

Simmer slowly, tightly covered, 20 minutes, then remove lid and cook, stirring, until nearly all liquid has evaporated. Cool thoroughly, at least 2 hours.

Prepare:

12 ounces beef suet

by cutting away any reddish or dry parts. Crumble the remainder, discarding as much of the papery filament as possible. You should have about 8 ounces, or 1 solidly packed cup. Freeze solid, then chop to a crumblike consistency or grind in a food processor. Combine with:

1½ cups (7.5 ounces) all-purpose flour

Rub lightly with your hands just until suet particles are separated. Add and rub until just blended:

1 cup (8 ounces) firmly packed dark brown sugar

1½ teaspoons ground cinnamon

1½ teaspoons ground ginger

½ teaspoon ground cloves

½ teaspoon salt

In a separate bowl, whisk together:

4 large eggs

⅓ cup (2.75 liquid ounces) brandy or cognac

⅓ cup (2.75 liquid ounces) cream sherry

Beat into the flour mixture, along with the cooked fruits and their juices. Add:

½ cup (3 ounces) finely chopped dates (optional)

¼ cup (2 ounces) finely chopped citron (optional)

To make a single large pudding, use either a 3-quart pudding mold or a deep, heatproof glass or ceramic bowl with a capacity of 12 to 14 cups. To make smaller puddings, use 2 to 3 molds and/or bowls with a total capacity of 3 to 4 quarts. Very thickly grease each mold with solid vegetable shortening, then pour in batter, leaving at least 1 inch of space between batter and the top of the mold. If the mold comes with a cover, grease the inside of the cover and snap it in place. Otherwise, crimp a sheet of foil over the rim of the mold, with little or no overhang down the sides, and cover foil with a plate, placed *upside-down*.

Arrange a rack or folded kitchen towel in the bottom of a large pot and set the mold(s) on top. Pour enough *boiling* water into the pot to come two-thirds up the sides of the mold(s). Cover the pot tightly. Bring water back to the boil over high heat, then adjust the heat to maintain the water at a brisk simmer, replenishing boiling water as necessary. Steam a large pudding for 3½ hours, two medium puddings for 2½ hours, and three small puddings for 2 hours. When done, the pudding(s) should be firm to the center and dark around the edges. (At this point, a large pudding may be left in the pot, *with the heat off,* for 3 hours, smaller puddings for about 1½ hours.) Using oven mitts, remove pudding(s) and let rest at room temperature for 20 minutes. Invert onto a platter to unmold. If you wish to flame the pudding, warm to barely tepid in a small saucepan:

½ cup (4 liquid ounces) brandy or cognac

Drizzle liquor over pudding, and then, standing back, ignite with a wooden match. Serve with:

hard sauce (below)

To store the pudding (it will become softer, darker, and more flavorful with age), cool to room temperature, then turn out of mold(s). Wrap first in plastic, then in foil and refrigerate for up to 1 month. To reheat, return pudding to original mold, well greased, and steam large pudding for 1½ to 2 hours, smaller puddings for 1 hour, or until a knife inserted in the center for 15 seconds comes out hot.

NOTE: Suet is the magic ingredient here, making the pudding soft, fine-grained, and moist. If possible, order it from a butcher: supermarket suet is intended primarily as bird food, and may not be genuine or fresh. Butter or shortening won't produce the same wonderful results.

HARD SAUCE

About 2½ cups (16 servings)

This sauce is called "hard" because it contains alcohol. Combine in a large bowl:

1 cup (8 ounces) unsalted butter, chilled but softened

3 cups (10 ounces) powdered sugar, sifted if lumpy

2 teaspoons vanilla

½ teaspoon freshly grated nutmeg

Beat at moderately high speed with an electric mixer until fluffy and pale but still thick enough to hold a firm shape, 6 to 10 minutes. Still beating, very slowly add:

¼ cup (2 liquid ounces) brandy, cognac, dark rum, or orange juice

Then add:

grated zest of 1 orange (optional)

Use at once, or store, tightly covered, in the refrigerator, for up to 3 days. Soften chilled sauce at room temperature until spreadable before transferring it to a serving bowl, or else it may deflate and thin out.

CANDIED CITRUS PEEL

About 2 cups

Delectable on its own, Candied Citrus Peel can also transform other desserts. For instance, it can be finely chopped and folded into cheesecake or gingerbread batters and even into ice cream! A tray set with Tuiles (French Almond Wafers), p. 37, and candied peel is dazzling with after-dinner coffee. For even more of a good thing, dip the candied peel in chocolate. This recipe is easily doubled.

Combine in a saucepan:

> peel of 3 oranges or 2 grapefruit or 6 lemons, in large strips
> water to cover

Simmer for 30 minutes. Drain, cover with cold water, and simmer until tender. Drain, refresh under cold water, and remove any remaining pulp or pith. Cut peel into strips ¼ inch wide and 2 inches long.

In a large heavy saucepan, stir over low heat until dissolved:

> 1 cup (7 ounces) sugar
> 3 tablespoons light corn syrup
> ¾ cup (6 liquid ounces) water

Dip a pastry brush in cold water and wash down the sides of the pan. Add fruit peel and cook very gently over low heat until most of the syrup has been absorbed. Cover and let stand overnight. Bring to a simmer again, then let cool a little and drain.

Spread several thicknesses of paper towel on a countertop and spread over it:

> 1 cup (7 ounces) sugar

Roll citrus peel in the sugar until well coated. Transfer the peel to a sheet of wax paper and let it air dry for at least 1 hour. To dip the peel in chocolate, melt chocolate as for Florentines Cockaigne, p. 43.

Holding each strip of peel at one end, dip into the melted chocolate. Transfer to another sheet of wax paper and let dry until chocolate is set.

Store, airtight, between layers of wax paper, in the refrigerator, for up to 4 months.

CANDIED ORANGE SLICES

About 3 dozen slices (1 pound)

Though not traditional, Candied Orange Slices make an imaginative addition to Christmas gift boxes. Try using half slices or chunks of fresh pineapple in place of the oranges.

Cut crosswise into ⅜-inch-thick slices, discarding the ends:

> 3 large (about 1 pound) seedless navel oranges

In a large heavy pan combine:

> 4½ cups (about 2 pounds) sugar
> 4 cups (32 liquid ounces) water

Using a long-handled wooden spoon, stir over low heat to dissolve the sugar. Raise the heat to medium and bring the mixture just to a boil. Brush down the sides of the pan with a damp pastry brush or wipe with a damp paper towel to prevent sugar from crystallizing.

Place the orange slices loosely overlapping on a rack, attach strings to it, and lower it into the pan. Press a round of wax paper on top. Bring syrup slowly to a simmer. Let simmer, without boiling, for 10 to 15 minutes. Remove the pan from the heat and let the oranges steep, covered, at room temperature for 24 hours.

Using the strings as handles, lift out the rack with the fruit on it and leave to drain, 30 minutes to 1 hour. Transfer the fruit peel to paper towels and leave until dry, 3 to 5 hours. The surface of the peel should be completely dry and hard.

Store, airtight, between layers of wax paper, at room temperature, for up to 1 week. Refrigerate for up to 3 weeks.

Facing photograph, top to bottom: Candied Citrus Peel, some dipped in chocolate, and Candied Orange Slices.

CHOCOLATE TRUFFLES   *About 30 1-inch truffles*

Black truffles, the kind found underground, are considered gourmet gold. These imitation chocolate ones are no less precious. Finished with a coating of finely grated chocolate and cocoa powder, these balls of solid chocolate are not at all complicated to assemble and look like the real thing.

In a medium microwave-safe bowl, place:

> 10 ounces bittersweet or semisweet chocolate, coarsely chopped

Microwave chocolate on 50 percent power for 1½ minutes, stirring halfway through. In a 2-cup glass measure, place:

> ⅔ cup (5.25 liquid ounces) heavy cream

Microwave the cream on high power until boiling, 2 to 3 minutes. Immediately pour the cream over the chocolate, stirring until the chocolate completely melts. (Alternatively, put the chocolate in a small deep bowl set in a warm place. In a medium saucepan, bring the cream to a boil over medium-high heat. Immediately pour the cream over the chocolate, stirring until the chocolate completely melts. If any chocolate pieces remain unmelted, set the bowl in a slightly larger bowl of hot water and stir until melted.)

Stir into mixture until well blended:

> 1½ tablespoons Grand Marnier, Kahlúa, cognac, or strong coffee

Cover and refrigerate the ganache mixture for at least 8 hours, or freeze, stirring frequently for about 1½ to 2 hours, until the mixture is very cold and stiff.

To form centers: Using a melon baller or teaspoon, scoop out about ¾-inch portions of the well-chilled chocolate mixture. Lightly roll each portion into a ball between the palms; balls do not have to be even. Lay on a wax paper–lined rimmed baking sheet. If the chocolate begins to build up on hands, wipe it off with paper towels. Also, if the chocolate becomes too soft to shape,

return to the refrigerator to firm up, then proceed. Lightly cover the baking sheet with plastic wrap and return to refrigerator until balls are firm, about 30 minutes.

To coat: In a food processor, grind until very fine:

> 2 ounces bittersweet or semisweet chocolate, coarsely chopped

Add:

> ½ tablespoon unsweetened cocoa

Process briefly to blend. Turn out into a small shallow bowl. One at a time, roll the truffles in coating mixture, turning to coat well.

Store, airtight, in a cool place for 1 week, or refrigerate for up to 3 weeks; allow to warm almost to room temperature before serving.

BOURBON BALLS   *About 60 1-inch balls (1 pound)*

Many of our readers don't think it's Christmas without this cherished *Joy* classic. These get even better as they age.

Sift together:

> 2 tablespoons unsweetened cocoa
>
> 1 cup (3.25 ounces) powdered sugar

In a separate bowl, whisk together until well mixed:

> ¼ cup (2 liquid ounces) bourbon whisky
>
> 2 tablespoons light corn syrup

Stir into cocoa mixture and set aside. In a food processor or electric mixer, crush:

> 2½ cups (10 ounces) crushed vanilla wafers

(Alternatively put wafers in a Ziploc bag and crush with a rolling pin or the bottom of a heavy saucepan.)

Mix with:

> 1 cup (4 ounces) coarsely chopped pecans

Stir vanilla wafers and pecans into cocoa mixture. Roll mixture into balls between palms (the balls do not have to be even). Roll in:

> ½ cup (1.75 ounces) powdered sugar

Store, airtight, for several weeks.

Facing photograph: Chocolate Truffles coated with chopped chocolate and cocoa and Bourbon Balls coated with powdered sugar.

PECAN BUTTERMILK PRALINES

2 dozen pralines (1½ pounds)

These are the authentic pralines found in New Orleans. It's the buttermilk that gives them their delectable tang. Preheat the oven to 350°F.

Spread in a baking pan and toast in the oven, stirring occasionally, 5 to 8 minutes, until very lightly browned:

> 2 cups (8 ounces) pecan halves or pieces

Set aside to cool.

Combine in a large heavy-duty saucepan:

> 1 cup (8 liquid ounces) buttermilk
> 2 cups (14 ounces) white sugar
> ½ cup (4 ounces) firmly packed golden brown sugar
> 1 teaspoon baking soda
> pinch of salt

Stir over low heat with a long-handled wooden spoon until the sugar is completely dissolved, about 5 minutes, then brush down the sides of the pan with a damp pastry brush or wipe with a damp paper towel to prevent the sugar from crystallizing.

Add:

> 4 tablespoons (2 ounces) unsalted butter, softened and cut into small pieces

Stir to melt the butter completely.

Raise the heat to medium, place a candy thermometer in the pan, and cook the mixture without stirring until it reaches the soft-ball stage, 236°F. Remove from the heat.

Quickly stir in the toasted pecans and:

> 1 teaspoon vanilla

Beat with a wooden spoon for about 1 minute, until the mixture begins to thicken and become opaque. Drop measuring tablespoonfuls onto a baking sheet lined with waxed paper or lightly buttered aluminum foil, forming patties about 2 inches in diameter. Let the pralines stand until completely cool, about 30 minutes. Store, airtight, at room temperature, between layers of wax paper, for several days.

BUTTERCRUNCH

About 2½ pounds

We searched long and hard for the perfect Buttercrunch recipe before finally finding this one.

Line a 10 x 15-inch jelly roll pan with heavy-duty aluminum foil, placing the foil shiny side up and allowing a 2-inch overhang at the two narrow ends of the pan. Coat foil with nonstick spray. Combine in a 3½-quart heavy pot or Dutch oven:

> 2⅓ cups (16.25 ounces) sugar
> ¾ cup (6 ounces) unsalted butter, cut in chunks
> ¼ cup (2 liquid ounces) light corn syrup
> 2 tablespoons water
> ½ teaspoon salt

Bring to a boil over high heat, stirring with a long-handled wooden spoon, then turn heat down to maintain mixture at a moderate simmer. Cook, stirring gently, until mixture turns a medium caramel color (325° on a candy thermometer), 5 to 8 minutes. Stir in:

> 1¼ cups (5.5 ounces) blanched slivered almonds
> 1¼ cups (5 ounces) coarsely chopped pecans or walnuts

Continue cooking until almonds turn a rich caramel brown, about 3 minutes. Be careful not to burn. Remove from heat and immediately stir in:

> 2 teaspoons vanilla

Working quickly, before mixture begins to harden, spread evenly in foil-lined pan with the back of a spoon. Transfer pan to a wire rack and let slab cool completely, about 1 hour. Peel off foil, then return slab to pan. Melt in a bowl set in hot water (or in a microwave at low power):

> 8 ounces bittersweet or semisweet chocolate

Pour chocolate over slab and spread evenly with a spatula or table knife. Immediately, before chocolate sets, sprinkle with:

> 1 cup (4 ounces) finely chopped nuts: half almonds and half walnuts or pecans, or some other combination

Pat lightly with your fingertips to imbed nuts without submerging them. Refrigerate slab until chocolate is cold and hard. While still cold, break slab into large chunks with your fingers.

Store, airtight, between layers of wax paper, in a cool place, but not the refrigerator, for up to 3 weeks.

Facing photograph: top and bottom, Pecan Buttermilk Pralines; left and right, Buttercrunch.

THE END

ACKNOWLEDGMENTS

Just as any holiday is a shared event, *Joy of Cooking Christmas Cookies* is a collective celebration of many individual talents and contributions. My deepest thanks go to Nancy Baggett, who truly sharpened the organization of the cookie section and made the techniques appealing to the contemporary cook—and who never minded our endless telephone calls, no matter what time of day or night. My heartfelt gratitude and respect go to Emily Luchetti, Alice Medrich, Stephen Schmidt, Selma Abrams, Mildred Kroll, Carole Bloom, Ginny Lawrence, Brigit Legere Binns, and Cindy Mushet for their assiduous work in retesting old and developing new recipes. A salute to Corby Kummer, author of *The Joy of Coffee*, for his expertise and precise information on coffee and chocolate.

Jackie Chwast's enchanting chapter-opening silhouette would have made Mom proud, as she herself created the silhouettes for the first editions of *Joy*. Laura Hartman Maestro's drawings are exquisite, and I consider it a great privilege to have her as our designated illustrator for the entire revision. Color pictures are a first for *Joy*, and Maura McEvoy's elegant photography adds a wonderfully festive beauty to these pages. I offer her my sincere thanks. No small thanks goes to food stylist Andrea Swenson, who meticulously slaved over each and every cookie in the photographs. Thanks also to Kemper Hyers of Edward Kemper Design for the props in the pictures.

At Simon & Schuster, thanks must go to Jack Romanos, Carolyn Reidy, Eric Rayman, and Jeff Wilson for providing the opportunity to make this book. At Scribner, my gratitude to Susan Moldow, Nan Graham, Roz Lippel, Theresa Horner, Marla Stutman, Pat Eisemann, and Bob Niegowski for their generous and unfailing support. Thanks also to the art and design team of Paula Scher at Pentagram, as well as Jackie Seow, John Fontana, Jenny Dossin, Amy Hill, and Katy Riegel, and Sam Potts for their creative vision; to Olga Leonardo for her production expertise; to Julie Primavera for a helping hand; and to M. C. Hald for her attention to words and detail.

The thanks and gratitude that go beyond words are due my editor, Maria Guarnaschelli, who is the very, very best that ever was at what she does! Many blessings on Marah Stets—and thanks for getting it done with a smile. Thanks to Kate Niedzwiecki, the assistant who really assists. To Gene Winick and Sam Pinkus my heartfelt thanks for the opportunity, support, and friendship, and who are also the very, very best. And to Susan, who plays Mozart in the morning.

INDEX